«For Immediate Release»

«For Immediate Release»

CANDIDATE PRESS RELEASES IN AMERICAN POLITICAL CAMPAIGNS

Jan Pons Vermeer

CONTRIBUTIONS IN POLITICAL SCIENCE, NUMBER 81

GREENWOOD PRESS
WESTPORT, CONNECTICUT • LONDON, ENGLAND

Library of Congress Cataloging in Publication Data

Vermeer, Jan Pons.
  "For immediate release".

  (Contributions in political science, ISSN 0147-1066;
no. 81)
    Bibliography: p.
    Includes index.
    1. Electioneering—United States. 2. Campaign
literature. 3. Press releases. I. Title. II. Series.
JK2281.V47   324.7'0973   81-20332
ISBN 0-313-22726-8 (lib. bdg.)   AACR2

Library of Congress Catalog Card Number: 81-20332
ISBN: 0-313-22726-8
ISSN: 0147-1066

First published in 1982

Greenwood Press
A division of Congressional Information Service, Inc.
88 Post Road West, Westport, Connecticut 06881

Printed in the United States of America

10 9 8 7 6 5 4 3 2 1

To my parents and my family

CONTENTS

TABLES AND FIGURES

TABLES

FIGURES

PREFACE

This book is written to demonstrate that campaign press releases are an efficient and reasonably inexpensive way for candidates to communicate with large segments of the electorate. Many candidates issue releases, quite a few newspapers use them regularly (and, it seems, more often than their editors would care to admit), and voters have substantial information available to them as a result. Yet releases do not command the respect their effectiveness warrants. Editors consider them public relations propaganda and little more. Politicians treat releases as a distinctly secondary (if not a tertiary) part of their campaigns. Frequently, in my conversations with some of them, I perceived their attitude about releases to be that "Releases are all right, but why not study 'real' campaigning?"

News releases are, of course, part of "real" campaigning, but the study of campaigning, coming into its own in the last decade or so, faces some real difficulties. Campaign materials are strangely evanescent; no sooner are they produced and used for their intended purpose than they disappear or become buried in mountains of records mixed with refuse. In the course of this research, I found campaign offices that disbanded without transferring the collected files to anyone; offices that still had copies of their releases, but no one had any idea where they were kept; and offices that kept their copies of releases in unorganized boxes filled with, to them, politically sensitive material, so no researcher was allowed near them, and no one else had the time to straighten out the mess. One breathes a grateful sigh, then, upon finding a well-organized campaign office.

Of course, a campaign office staff has better things to do during the hectic final months of a campaign than organize records; that is not the point. If, however, studies of campaigns are to move beyond the impressionistic, anecdotal accounts produced by those who have had actual experience in a campaign to systematic studies of limited aspects of campaigns, appropriate research materials are needed. Studies of campaign expenditures have expanded our knowledge of the role and use of money in campaigns tremendously in the last several years, but those studies have been possible because candidates have been required to submit detailed records. One can only hope that something can be done to aid systematic research of other aspects of campaigning; perhaps a center can be established where campaign documents can be sent when a campaign wants to dispose of its files. Such a campaign materials archive could then allow researchers access to the material under appropriate safeguards, most notably a guarantee of nonpolitical use of the information.

Until such a systematic method of gaining access to materials is established, campaign research is going to proceed slowly, perhaps haphazardly. I have been fortunate in finding several campaigns with excellent records to which I have been allowed access. But one is never satisfied; more releases and more clipping files would have been helpful.

Because so many have helped, singling some out of the many for thanks may insult those omitted. No one will feel slighted, however, if I acknowledge the intellectual debt I owe Stanley Kelley Jr., and the substantial assistance of J. Fred Coldren in the early stages of this study. The help of Nebraska Wesleyan University in the form of an E. C. Ames Faculty Fellowship made a tremendous difference, and I never could have tamed the computer at Wesleyan had it not been for the patience, skill, and dexterity of that bearded historian, Ronald C. Naugle. The long-distance leg work of Trudy Selleck, who kept insisting that "This is not work—it's fun," was indispensable. Recognizing the aid of others, however, is not a sneaky way of avoiding the blame for the errors that may occur in the pages that follow; since it's my name on the title page, all of the errors are mine as well.

«For Immediate Release»

1

REACHING VOTERS WITH NEWS RELEASES

The victory of Brendan T. Byrne, the Democratic candidate for governor of New Jersey, over his Republican opponent, Charles W. Sandman, Jr., on November 6, 1973, was, in one sense, a surprise. Less than a year before, Byrne was virtually unknown in the state, while Sandman, in part because of two previous unsuccessful attempts to win the Republican gubernatorial nomination, enjoyed much wider public recognition. But by late October, it was a foregone conclusion that Byrne would defeat Sandman and do so by a comfortable margin; Sandman received only 617,801 votes to 1,307,983 for Byrne.[1] This turn of events, which made a political unknown the governor-elect of a populous state, came about because of fortuitous political circumstances (widespread corruption in the administration of incumbent William T. Cahill gave Democrats a chance, and the absence of a clear-cut leading Democratic candidate gave Byrne his opportunity), but it took a long political campaign to clinch the victory. The Byrne campaign managed to introduce its candidate to New Jersey voters in such a way that the majority of them decided to vote for him.

The problem the Byrne campaign faced is typical. Campaigns require candidates to persuade voters to support them, which depends on their success in disseminating information about the candidate, his position on the issues, and his opponent. "Right or wrong," John Kingdon wrote, "most candidates believe that campaigns affect election outcomes."[2] Like the Byrne campaign, other campaigns expend tremendous resources and energy to influence voters' choices.

In essence, campaigns are exercises in communication.[3] They are vehicles for communicating with voters in order to influence them. As Walter De Vries and Lance Tarrance correctly argued, "the campaign process is best understood as an information and communications system."[4] The new campaign methods, which take advantage of recently developed technology, may have altered campaign organizations by bringing in consultants with different backgrounds and expertise, but they have not changed the basic nature and purpose of campaigning: communicating with voters.[5]

A variety of ways to communicate with voters is available to candidates, each with characteristic advantages and disadvantages; there are no easy choices here, unfortunately. Limited financial resources force many campaigners to choose among these means, rather than use them all. Getting the optimal mix of these communication alternatives—billboards and buttons, television and newspapers, pamphlets and radio—is what campaign strategy is about.

Two main criteria by which candidates choose methods of communication involve access to voters and control over the messages sent. Campaigners tend to choose methods that reach more potential voters per unit cost and prefer techniques that give them greater control over the content. But techniques that give them the greatest control, such as television spot commercials, can be easily identified as candidate propaganda, which causes many voters to raise their guards; this access is not worth as much.[6] On the other hand, campaign communication through means not controlled by the candidate, such as press reports of public appearances, leaves the content of the message available to the voters under the control of others; thus those messages may not convey what the candidate wants the voters to know. The two criteria are interrelated. The message on the billboard may tell voters exactly what the candidates want them to learn, but it may reach fewer voters than a newscast reporting a speech by the candidate. Both criteria are important in this study, although the notion of control plays a larger part in the framework developed here.

In fact, campaigners send messages through both controlled and uncontrolled channels. They have good reasons for not limiting their efforts to controllable channels. Means of communication that are totally under campaign control are not as likely to be effective in persuading voters as are uncontrolled means, because voters are less likely to see the latter as biased. For that reason, as Charles

Smith commented in 1948, "party publicity directors . . . agree that the best propaganda is that which does not appear as propaganda. Getting into the news columns is better than inserting advertisements."[7] The undecided voter and the ticket-splitter are more likely to respond favorably to sources of information such as television newscasts than to newspaper advertisements. "Thus any major campaign communication effort directed toward the ticket-splitter must go through media that cannot be completely controlled (i.e., purchased) by the candidates."[8] Also, most voters get more campaign information from the news media and from contacts with friends and coworkers than from candidate-controlled sources.[9] Daniel Gaby and Merle Treusch offered candidates this observation:

In all but the smallest electorate subdivision, you cannot expect to meet every possible voter. That means a vast majority of the people you need to win will have no contact with you except for the media.[10]

Giving up control over some campaign communications is a necessary part of campaigning. Simply put, candidates cannot reach enough voters through controlled channels to win the election. Reaching otherwise inaccessible voters is worth the risk of giving others control over campaign messages.

Campaign techniques that give others significant control over the content of the communications available to voters are different in one important way from techniques that involve direct communication with voters or techniques that are subject to total campaign control. The difference is simply that the latter techniques need satisfy only the requirements that the campaigners might have for them; the former techniques, however, must satisfy some intermediaries before the voters can be reached with the message, intermediaries who may judge the communication by wholly different standards. The criteria these intermediaries apply have an unavoidable impact; the result is that the choice of a channel of communication is rarely uncomplicated. The transmittal by an intermediary—to the extent the intermediary has some discretion about whether to send the message on or about the way in which to send the message—of campaign communication means that the standards and preferences of the intermediary are involved.[11]

An example may pin down the distinction. When considering an advertisement, campaigners need take into account mainly the possible reactions of those likely to be exposed to it—they can be assured that their advertisement will be printed if they can pay the bill.[12] But if the candidate wants to explain his position on a particular issue, he may find an advertisement inadequate (too little time, for instance, in which to make the explanation). He may therefore arrange to speak to an appropriate audience, hoping that reporters present will write a news story on his position and that editors will give the story prominent play in the next edition of the papers. The candidate will have reached one audience—the people who heard his speech—directly, but whether his position on the issue in question becomes widely known depends mainly on reporters and editors. However, the candidate has no way of insuring favorable treatment of this position by the newspapers. The impact of his speech and the success of his message, therefore, depend on the intermediaries and on whether the message meets their criteria.

Candidates, however, have learned not to leave such matters solely to the whims of others. Several techniques designed to increase a candidate's control over the messages reaching the voters have been developed. The media event is a widely known technique of this sort. The proper visual background for making a statement, conventional wisdom suggests, increases the likelihood that the statement will be reported on television newscasts. "McGovern," Timothy Crouse reported, "would spend a whole morning hauling the press corps to some farm in the Midwest just so that he could appear against a background of grain silos when he made a statement about the wheat scandal."[13] The candidate stages his pronouncement so that the criteria television news producers use to select items for the newscasts are met. Although, as Conrad Joyner pointed out, "it is obvious that pseudo-events lack spontaneity and are staged or encouraged by skillful men for the purpose of being reported,"[14] media events get widespread television coverage. It is a good deal for the candidate. He makes his statement to a large audience, often on all three networks; he increases his control over the message the voters receive.

Candidates also issue campaign press releases to exercise more control over the messages voters receive. From presidential campaigns to campaigns for minor local offices, virtually all candidates make news releases available.[15] Why? Harold V. Hunter, state chairman of the Oklahoma Republican party, said it is because with releases, a candidate "can keep control." He suggested that "control is most important," and that campaign press releases help provide that control.[16] Candidates also issue releases, because the news coverage that may result is less likely to be seen as candidate inspired. The stories in the press often do not identify the source of the material. Furthermore, as Gaby and Treusch told candidates, "this kind of exposure in the media is almost free. While there are some out-of-pocket costs you'll incur . . . , these are minimal compared to the value of the coverage."[17] The access at a reasonable cost to voters unaware that they are targets of propaganda, coupled with the ability to influence what the press prints, makes press releases worthwhile.

Releases can increase a candidate's control over news coverage in three ways. First, they may stimulate coverage in newspapers that otherwise would not be able to run a story on a particular campaign development. Small dailies and most weeklies, for example, can rarely afford to assign a full-time reporter to campaign news. A campaign press release, if available, might be printed by newspapers that have no other sources for that story. (In this instance, releases are also a way in which candidates can keep reporters and editors up to date on their campaigns.) In addition, reporters often combine campaign press releases with other news. Without the release, the story would have run anyway, but if the reporter has the release available, he may decide to augment his item with material from the release. Releases that might not warrant a story for themselves may still find their way into print in this way. Also, the content of the release may influence the way in which reporters respond to the event they are covering. Some of the emphasis on certain elements of such events in press releases may find its way into the reporters' stories, if only because they provide concrete evidence of the candidate's position.[18] Releases can, then, help editors and reporters cover campaigns, and campaign news releases help candidates get good news coverage, because reporters and editors find releases helpful.

Both editors and politicians minimize the importance and impact of campaign press releases, but the widespread use of releases warrants a different assessment. Candidates distribute press releases, because newspapers use them. For some candidates, those running for a minor local office, for instance, campaign press releases may provide the only feasible way to obtain coverage during the campaign. They would be unrealistic to expect to draw reporters to media events and press conferences. Even campaigns with a strong orientation toward the electronic media issue releases. The results, for campaigners, are often gratifying. It is simple for them to verify the use of their releases for themselves, since they can scan the local press the days after they issue a release to see whether it was used and how it was treated. Campaign manuals encourage candidates to issue releases and most include a section to instruct those unfamiliar with the details on how to write and issue releases.[19]

This optimistic appraisal of press use of campaign releases is reinforced by the little research that has been done on the question. Lynda Lee Kaid found that 69 percent of one candidate's releases were used by at least one paper in his district, and John Bolen reported that most of the releases issued by two candidates for governor of Texas in 1970 resulted in some press coverage.[20] Hunter, the Oklahoma party official quoted earlier, pointed out that even if only one out of every ten campaign releases is used by the press, releases are an "effective" means of reaching voters.[21] The data to be reported in this study are in line with these results: campaign press releases are widely used by newspapers.

It is, of course, also indisputable that quite a few releases do not find their way into print and that many of those that are used have their messages diluted or even eliminated. Issuing a press release is no guarantee of coverage. The crux of the matter is a conflict of standards. Journalists have criteria by which they judge the appropriateness of news releases that are to some extent incompatible with the requirements of a good campaign release from the perspective of a campaigner. Although editors look for hard news content, campaigners issue releases even when there is no hard news.[22] Editors want a good journalistic style, and campaigners prefer a style capable of persuading voters. Editors prefer impartial treatment of the event reported, but candidates need reports favorable to their side. But if campaigners want newspapers to use their releases, and if they want to exercise as much control as possible over the final product appearing in the press, they must comply with editorial standards; not to do so is to waste time and effort with releases.

One would expect, then, that candidates who issue press releases would write them with this difficulty in mind. Their task is to sneak their campaign propaganda past the watchful eyes of the press' gatekeepers.[23] Ralph Casey pointed out that "parties found that they could get their propaganda into newspaper columns by dressing it up in interesting clothes," and he is partially correct.[24] Interesting clothes is the right idea, but it is not enough. Campaigners should provide a reason for covering a campaign event compelling enough so that the editor will not want to pass it up and a format for covering it that the editor will find convenient to use and professionally acceptable in style.

My purpose in this study is to explore the general problem of communication by candidates with voters through channels controlled by intermediaries by examining campaign press releases and their use. The problems that campaigners who use press releases face are similar to the problems faced by those who stage media events, call press conferences to get media exposure, and use any communication technique that depends on the assent and cooperation of others. The "what" in Harold Lasswell's famous description of the communication process—"Why says what to whom with what effect?"—must be altered to fit the research question I am concerned with—how does the participation of intermediaries influence "what" campaigners try to communicate and "what" newspaper readers finally have available to them?[25] Since a great deal of political communication passes through such channels, the conclusions drawn here have wider implications.[26]

Campaign press releases are an appropriate example of this type of communication to study, because releases are so widely issued, and because the standards editors apply to them can be relatively easily determined, in part because of the tremendous volume of self-criticism in which journalists have been engaged in the last decade.[27]

This study deals with the press releases issued by a number of campaigns ranging from those for offices such as county board of supervisors to the president of the United States. Much of what we can learn from these campaigns is used to amplify results gleaned from a larger scale study of one campaign and its releases in particular: the gubernatorial campaign between Brendan T. Byrne and Charles W. Sandman, Jr., in New Jersey in 1973. Byrne and Sandman showed what can be done with campaign press releases in a first-class press operation. Their campaign fits the purpose; it is appropriate as a keystone for this study for five reasons. First, since no incumbent was in the race, Sandman having defeated incumbent Cahill in the June primary, neither candidate could claim the resources of incumbency, including the added claim on media attention an incumbent can easily press.[28] Incumbency can distort a study of campaign press releases, sometimes because incumbents can issue a large number of "nonpolitical" releases during a campaign, and sometimes because incumbents limit their releases during a campaign, as Congressman J. J. Pickle (D-Tex.) did during his 1978 reelection campaign.[29] Second, the race was for a significant office. The governorship is one of the top political prizes available in any state. A race for such an office is likely to attract quite a bit of attention from the news media; yet neither candidate wanted to rely on the coverage the press would provide on its own initiative.

Third, New Jersey gubernatorial elections take place in odd-numbered years, when neither Congress nor the president is up for election. The absence of competing elections is a significant factor, because candidates frequently have to compete with candidates for other offices for coverage as well as with the opponent. But during the Byrne-Sandman campaign, no presidential candidates were criss-crossing the state or being written about in the press. No senatorial candidates tried to speak for the entire state. No congressional candidates were flooding newspapers with requests for coverage. The gubernatorial campaign was the major political story.

Fourth, because New Jersey has no commercial VHF television station of its own, press coverage becomes that much more important to candidates and the public under these conditions.[30] Philadelphia, New York City, and Wilmington are the major television markets, but they serve a predominantly non-New Jersey audience. Because these stations have little incentive to provide much news and public affairs coverage of New Jersey, they are not a very good independent source of information for New Jersey voters. The situation is comparable to that faced by candidates whose districts comprise only part of the area served by local television stations. They, too, must rely on other means of communication with voters, and the press is often a worthwhile alternative. As Peter Clarke and Eric Fredin reported, "the public relies on newspapers somewhat more than on television for political news."[31]

Finally, the New Jersey press is an active, vibrant press, including thriving dailies and well-read weeklies.[32] New Jersey papers differ enough from one another for us to expect to see differences in their treatment of campaign news releases, and they are active enough to make it likely that their editors will want to provide better news coverage than the competition. For all of these reasons, the Byrne and Sandman campaign makes a worthwhile centerpiece for this study; if campaign press releases can be an effective part of campaigns, the Byrne and Sandman case will show it. Detailed references to other campaigns round out the study.

An additional factor makes the Byrne-Sandman contest interesting to examine. The two candidates were different. One was virtually unknown before the campaign started, had never served in an elective office, and did not have a public record of past votes on political issues to defend. The other had run statewide campaigns before, had served in the state legislature and in Congress for seventeen years, and had a public record to defend. Byrne was widely viewed as a liberal, while Sandman flaunted his conservatism. These differences called for different strategies and made it plausible that the two candidates would issue releases with different content and that editors would respond to the releases in different ways, depending in part on how they felt about the candidates and about the issues and about the issues raised in the releases.

The central concern of this study is the way in which newspapers treated the campaign press releases candidates sent them. To the extent that the releases were used and to the extent that they were used largely as they were written, the releases provided the candidates with an efficient means of communicating with voters despite the ultimate control over the process exercised by editors and reporters. Just how effective a means of voter communication the releases were for Sandman and Byrne, as well as for the other candidates to be considered, is a question to be answered below. A study of this scope has rarely been attempted. Most examinations of press releases either have dealt with relatively minor races or have involved mainly the way the press used the releases without putting the releases into the context of the campaign. To that extent, this study is unique.

Journalists seem to use certain criteria to distinguish between events worth reporting as news and other events, and the press seems to play three roles—news seeker, truth seeker, and adversary of government. These roles and criteria suggest four standards for judging how the press handles candidate releases: how accurately the release is handled, how complete the story based on the release is, whether the treatment is impartial, and whether relevant background information is provided. The results show that, in general, the nation's press and New Jersey's press in particular met these standards.

The results of the study indicate that news releases are an effective campaign tool. Even though editors and reporters can reject press releases or change them to suit their own purposes, thereby diluting or distorting a candidate's point, quite a few newspapers publish releases with little or no changes. The advantages for campaigners are enormous. The resulting news stories are rarely identified as candidate inspired, and the releases reach a potentially large audience despite the relatively low cost of preparing and distributing them. For voters, the results are not so pleasing. They gain access to information the candidate wants them to have, but they are seldom told about the source of the news story, something that is important for them to know to evaluate it correctly.

For journalists, the results are not as surprising. Most of them know that releases are a significant part of campaign coverage. Political campaigns are news, and journalists will cover campaign developments, whether or not candidates provide press releases and other aids. But since candidates want to maximize their coverage and want to stimulate favorable stories about themselves, they will hold press conferences, stage media events, and issue releases. Because journalists have been receptive to such candidate-inspired news, reports based on these events will continue to appear in the press. It is in large part because of the nature of journalism that campaign press releases are successful.

2

GUARDIANS OF THE CHANNEL

The flow of political information in any political system to those who seek it in order to make intelligent decisions is idiosyncratic. Exactly who receives which piece of information depends perhaps more on the structures and institutions that handle the distribution of information for the society than on the initiatives of message senders and information seekers. Walter Lippmann noted in 1922 that political information is not automatically or even easily made available to the public. Instead of frequent face-to-face contact between candidate and voter or between policymaker and citizen, the contact is usually indirect (despite the fact that modern technology and travel allow candidates and officials to meet many more persons than their counterparts of earlier years could). Lippmann said, "It is assumed that the press should do spontaneously for us what primitive democracy imagined each of us could do spontaneously for himself."[1] Since individuals cannot obtain the information they need by themselves, and since candidates and officials cannot provide the facts and interpretations of those facts they would like the public to have directly, both the public and newsmakers are likely to use the channels provided by the media. These channels include the electronic media, such as television and radio, and the print media, of which the press is the most important.[2]

In years past, and in other nations, candidates or parties and government officials have taken major steps to provide the public with the facts that they deemed it desirable they should have. Early newspapers in the United States were little more than party organs, providing its readers with interpretations (from their perspective) of current political events. In the United States, a government news-paper never developed (although the federal government spends a great deal of money on publicity and publications), but in other nations, both in the western and non-western worlds, official and semiofficial government newspapers flourish. If media do not exist, it seems candidates and government officials will create their own.

Although the distribution of political information among citizens is important in any society, in the case of democracy, it is indispensable to its existence. A democratic political system presupposes a public well informed enough to make decisions on candidates and policies. Thomas Schroth commented, "Democracy in the United States could not operate without this role of communicator played by the press."[3] James Reston agreed; the press provides news, and "the news consists of all facts which, in a democracy, the people must have in order to reach correct and sound judgments on the conduct of their public affairs."[4]

It has been argued that the First Amendment to the Constitution, which prohibits Congress from infringing on the freedom of the press, was intended in part to allow the press to play this vital role in the American system by protecting the flow of information to the public from undue interference by government. Fred S. Siebert referred to the libertarian theory of the press, which, he said, is embodied in the First Amendment.[5] He argued that the "founders of the American system of government held the political function of the press to be paramount," and that one of the main activities of the press was to provide the means "by which the general public received information and discussion on matters of public importance."[6] George Anastaplo argued that "the First Amendment acknowledges that the sovereign citizen has the right freely to discuss public business."[7] Justice William Brennan noted in *New York Times Company* v. *Sullivan* that "the general proposition that freedom of expression upon public questions is secured by the First Amendment has long been settled."[8]

Given that importance to the functioning of the democratic system, the way in which the press performs its vital communication function can make a great deal of difference to the decisions the public reaches. Since not everything that takes place can be reported, what the public learns about public affairs depends to a large extent on what the newspapers pass along. Lippmann, again, made the point succinctly:

Every newspaper when it reaches the reader is the result of a whole series of selections as to what items shall be printed, in what positions they shall be printed, how much space each shall occupy, what emphasis each shall have.[9]

Such decisions are not neutral. Paul Weaver noted that:

A citizen's perception, thought, and action concerning public matters are invariably altered as a result of learning about them through news rather than through conversation or direct observation or some other means.[10]

By its freedom to report what it wishes and by its freedom to treat what it reports as it wishes, the press itself influences the substance of what is communicated from newsmakers to the public. Recent research has suggested, too, that the press has a substantial impact on the public's judgment about which issues are important among those under public discussion."[11] To understand the actions and choices of the public and to understand the attempts by newsmakers to communicate with the public through the medium of the press, one must take into account the influence of the channel itself on the message.

The notion involved here is that of the gatekeeper. By the choices reporters and editors make to determine which events will be reported, they control access to the newspaper columns.[12] The upshot is that communication between official and public, to the extent that it passes through the press, is subject to the discretion of reporters, editors, and publishers. The decisions about what the public needs to know to play its proper role in a democracy are not made by the public itself or by public officials (except insofar as they too select which things to say or not to say), but rather by the gatekeeper who controls access to the press.

It is therefore important, if we want to say anything significant about candidate communication with voters through press releases, to consider communication between officials and the public through the press in general. The way in which newspaper reporters and editors treat press releases is but one example of the way in which they deal with the many demands for space in the next edition of the paper.

It seems tautological, and almost trivial, to say that the main function of the press, of newspapers, is to seek and report the news.

A glance at any recent issue of virtually any newspaper, however, will show that most of the available space is devoted to matters other than news. Features, comics, financial and personal advice, advertising, and so forth take up most of the space. Furthermore, it is not at all clear what is meant when one speaks of "news." A comparison of different newspapers will often remind us that what one editor considers worth printing, another may not consider newsworthy at all.

Standards for what is and is not news are relatively ambiguous and only imperfectly shared among journalists. Bernard Cohen noted that "reporters have great difficulty in putting into words just what they are hunting for each day."[13] The ambiguity of the press's standards of news is only part of the problem. In addition, journalists often fail to distinguish between the event that may be reported and the report of the event itself. Warren Breed, for example, does not make that distinction. He defined news as "the reports of a recent event (or situation?) judged by newsmen to be worthy of publication for the interest and/or information of members of their audience."[14] But if news is the report, rather than the event, we run into circular reasoning. An event is not news until it has been reported; once an event has been reported as news, it *is* news, whether or not the reporter made a correct judgment about the news values involved. "[News] takes on a kind of objective reality: what was reported is news; what was not reported—for whatever reasons—is not news."[15]

If there is a way out of this quandary, a path to lead to a firmer notion of what reporters seek to report as news, it may be in recognizing the characteristics that reporters and analysts seem to agree that newsworthy events have in common. Many writers have compiled lists of such factors. The rationale behind them is the idea that the intuitive judgment a reporter makes about the newsworthiness of a particular occurrence is usually the same as the judgment of another reporter—news people seem to decide in the same way whether an event is worth reporting. Such implicit judgments can perhaps be made explicit by listing the characteristics that newsworthy events share.[16] Five characteristics that many such lists include, which also are crucial to distinguishing news from other events, are timeliness, conflict, impact, unexpectedness, and the involvement of important people. Of course, no list of newsworthy characteristics can be exhaustive; this one certainly is not. The

point is that events including one or more of these five characteristics are more likely to be covered by reporters, to the extent that
reporters become aware or are made aware of such events.

News is timely; an event is no longer newsworthy if it is not relatively promptly reported. Although the advent of the electronic
media, which can communicate a startling development long before
a special edition of a newspaper can hit the streets, has superseded
the competition between papers in the same town to see who can
report the latest developments first, news people still emphasize
the most recent reports. The wire service reporters, representing
the Associated Press, United Press International, and other such
associations, have almost constant deadlines. They file updated
stories throughout the day, eager to beat each other even by minutes.
Timothy Crouse noted:

There was only one type of reporter who dashed for the phones at almost
every [campaign] stop and called in bulletins about almost everything that
happened on the schedule. That was the wire service reporter.[17]

But other reporters are concerned with the recency of the events
they report as well. As Delmer D. Dunn pointed out, "News is a
perishable commodity."[18]

A second characteristic of news is that it involves conflict. If
there is a dispute among newsmakers or if there is a disagreement
about policy, it is news. As E. E. Schattschneider pointed out in
another context, "Nothing attracts a crowd so quickly as a fight.
Nothing is so contagious."[19] Stories about conflict, like conflict
itself, draw attention and draw interest. Reporters search out potential, hidden, or covert conflict among participants in a policy decision, and when they find such conflict, they often make it the
central point of their stories, their lead. The implication is that the
real news is where the conflict is. It points to the area of policy
that was most difficult to agree upon and where agreement may
break down most quickly. Furthermore, it indicates that there is
disagreement on the impact of the policy—that some think it will
hurt and others think it will help. It is clear, however, that the tendency of reporters to focus their attention on conflict may distort
their news stories. They may, for example, stress a relatively insignificant difference between two candidates in a debate over
garbage-collection procedures and pass over virtually without com-

ment the fact that the two candidates agree on important matters such as the feasibility of a city income tax.[20]

Newsworthy events have an impact, either a large impact on relatively few people or a lesser impact on a large number of people.[21] A fire in a tenement, with its tremendous impact on the lives of the people who reside there, or a development in tax-reform legislation, with its influence on the financial affairs of a large number of people, are examples of events that are newsworthy because of their impact. The effect need not be immediate—it may be potential. Nor need it be obvious—it may be latent. But occurrences with such impact are worth reporting.

News contains surprises. An unexpected event, statement, development, or occurrence is more likely to be reported as news. The exceptional happening, whether a plane crash or the development of a cancer cure, falls into this category. Another way of formulating this notion is to label it "change." Dunn, for instance, used change as an essential characteristic of news: "A new course of action, a departure in a *new or unexpected* direction, or a difference from past practices is likely to be considered newsworthy by a reporter."[22] If nothing has changed, or has changed only in expected directions, there is no news; such events are unlikely to spark the interest of the public. Reporters are well aware of that fact.

A last characteristic of newsworthy events is that they involve noteworthy people. Cohen reported that foreign correspondents think that " 'big names' make news."[23] Dunn noted that "reporters believe that people are interested in what the top officials say and do. The 'bigger' the name, the more newsworthy are the events with which the name is associated."[24] Noteworthy people are often those who have done something worth reporting in the past. Such past associations with a newsworthy occurrence make such people newsworthy for future events as well. Herbert Gans called them "Knowns"; "Some are assumed by journalists to be familiar names among the audience; others have appeared frequently in the news and are therefore well known to the journalists."[25] This characteristic, then, becomes almost circular—what a person who has made news in the past does is more likely to be reported as news than what another person does. The former is then more likely again to be able to draw the attention of the press, because he has become newsworthy.

In summary, journalists seek out and report recent, unexpected events involving important people in conflicts that have a great or potentially great impact. The more of these five characteristics a development may involve, the more likely it is that newspapers will report it. Journalists use these criteria not only because they are the standards of their profession, but also because they are convinced that these criteria identify the developments their audience wants to read and hear about. There is no guarantee, of course, that reporters will learn about all instances where news, according to these criteria, is being made. But when they are aware of them, and when they have the time and resources to do so, reporters are more likely to report events with more of these characteristics than those with fewer of them. Since space is limited, editors will use the same criteria to choose among stories, but tailor the criteria to fit the particular readership of their papers.

What is reported as news is not necessarily all true. Lippmann's classic distinction between news and truth deserves repetition: "The function of news is to signalize an event, the function of truth is to bring to light the hidden facts, to set them into relation with each other, and make a picture of reality on which men can act."[26]

The classic illustration of the difficulty for readers of newspapers to determine the truth, given the ways news is presented, is the publicity that former Senator Joseph McCarthy of Wisconsin received for his "Communists in government" allegations in the early 1950s.[27] Senator McCarthy was a noteworthy person (made more so after his accusations showered him with publicity) whose charges, if true, involved matters that would affect millions of people a great deal—the security of the national government and perhaps the survival of the nation were imperiled. His charges were therefore newsworthy, and they were duly reported. It turned out that his allegations were never substantiated. The "picture of reality" readers of newspapers got was at variance with the actual situation. The State Department, for instance, was not riddled with Communists. Richard Rovere noted that reporters covering McCarthy were "angry about the system that required them to publish 'news' they knew to be fraudulent but prohibited them from reporting their knowledge of its fraudulence."[28] The guidelines of objective reporting make it difficult for reporters to report news and present a truthful "picture of reality" at the same time.

When a reporter plays the role of truth seeker, his values, preferences, and potential bias may intrude. He may be less than "objective" in his reporting. Objectivity in reporting is related to the conception of the medium as a transmitter of messages from a source to a receiver. The medium should, ideally, exert no influence over this transmission that would change the impression the receiver obtains from that which he would have gotten had the message been communicated directly. The medium must be neutral. This notion of objectivity has long been almost a fetish for news people, but the McCarthy (and other) episode(s) made it clear that objective reporting can be inconsistent with truth telling. Objectivity requires reporters to treat false and misleading statements the same way they treat factual and forthright statements, to the detriment of the reader who must rely on the reporter for a realistic picture of what transpired.

Dissatisfaction with objectivity in reporting has increased. Timothy Crouse quoted Brit Hume on the subject:

[Reporters] claim that they're trying to be objective. They shouldn't try to be objective, they should try to be honest. And they're *not* being honest. Their so-called objectivity is just a guise for superficiality. They report what one candidate said, then they go and report what the other candidate said with equal credibility. They never get around to find out if the guy is telling the truth. They just pass the speeches along without trying to confirm the substance of what the candidates are saying. What they pass off as objectivity is just a mindless kind of neutrality.[29]

Congressman Richard Bolling, from the point of view of a news source, commented to the same effect:

The concept of objectivity, superficially plausible, rules out the informed interpretation, the "in-depth" piece that explains why such a vote is meaningful and how Representative X's voting record on a given issue may be keyed to certain pressure groups.[30]

The effect on reporters themselves should not be minimized. Joel Swerdlow described how the canons of objectivity affected the reporting by news people assigned to cover the 1980 Reagan-Carter campaign:

. . . a full week before election day, the pack sensed that Carter was finished, but rules of objectivity prevented them from reporting it. They were too bound—and sometimes blinded—by the polls, by presumed truths emanating from their desks, and by the cynicism bred from isolation and daily repetition of self-serving exaggerations by the candidates. A desperate search for something newsworthy had worn away the fine edges of their political judgment.[31]

Journalists have been increasingly uncomfortable with the restraints that objectivity puts on them.

Yet the profession as a whole still shares "the assumption that objective and unbiased reporting of events is possible and desirable and that the sphere of politics in any society can be best observed from a neutral or non-partisan perspective."[32] But in one of the best analyses of objective reporting written so far, Bernard Roshco suggested that "much of the difficulty in dealing with the question of objective reporting lies in the confusion between bias and objectivity."[33] Traditionally, newspaper reporters have attempted to avoid their biases in reporting the news by refusing to bring to bear any information for which they could not get "institutional sources for authoritative confirmation."[34] But in restricting his sources of information so much, the reporter not only kept out his biases, but also decreased the possibility of reporting an accurate picture of reality; he substituted someone else's biases for his own. As a result, journalists did not report news objectively at all. They actually reported news contaminated with unrecognized and therefore unacknowledged and uncontrolled biases, biases that readers had no way of being aware of.

Objective reporting cannot provide newspaper readers with the information necessary to understand and interpret the events being reported; interpretation of events is required. As Dan Nimmo put it, "The responsibility of the newsman is 'truth-telling' for society, and, for the political community, it is the telling of political truths."[35] To tell such truths, a reporter must often go beyond what official and authoritative sources provide him. He must be able to bring to bear his own experience and to draw conclusions from what might otherwise be a series of unconnected facts. Ben Bagdikian made the point in his usual direct style:

The role of the news media is not merely to report like a tape recorder whatever someone in authority choose to say in public. . . . Newspapers, radio-TV, and magazines should scan the social horizon and make their own decisions about what is important, independent of officialdom. If the President chooses not to talk about issues, this does not mean that objective journalists are forbidden to describe and illuminate the issues. If what is

said officially is contradicted by what was said earlier, good journalists
are supposed to have memories.[36]

If the press is to play a useful role in providing information for
public decisions, it must do more than report. It must seek the
truth; it must interpret the news. In other words, the press should
be more than "neutral finders and conveyers of information."[37]
But if this role leads reporters to add to what they learn from
their news sources when necessary, it can be safely assumed that the
sources in question will often feel as if the press is against them,
that the press is biased, and that the press is an enemy. These feelings are likely to be closest to the surface when the newsmakers
are in a position in which they need to use the press to communicate
with the public, be it the people as a whole, a particular constituence,
or potential voters. Interpretive reporting makes it more difficult
for the public figure to communicate a specific message, because
the message may be diluted, distorted, disregarded, or redefined
by the reporter. Dunn concluded that "the more reporters act in
accordance with the neutral ideal, the more control officials exercise
over the content of messages transmitted about government."[38]
Public officials and candidates will prefer the press to be merely
"neutral finders and conveyers of information," because such a
role serves their purposes best. But the growing emphasis on interpretive reporting casts the press and newsmakers into two opposing
groups and marks yet a third role for the press: that of critic of
the government.

Fred Siebert argued that the libertarian theory of the press, which
seems to describe the American press rather well, despite hints of a
developing trend of social responsibility, requires the press to be a
"check on government." The press is "charged with the duty of
keeping government from overstepping its bounds."[39] That duty
makes the press an adversary of government.[40] The notion is widely
accepted. Dunn reported that "the literature is replete with references to the conflict between reporters and public officials,"[41] and
he is right. For instance, Elmer Cornwell, in discussing the press
and the president, pointed out:

Clearly the relation of press to White House is an antagonistic one. Their
divergent goals produce frictions inasmuch as what one wants concealed
the other wants to expose, and estimates of newsworthiness are bound
to diverge often.[42]

Recently, Michael Grossman and Martha Kumar, although not denying the adversary element, suggested that the relationship between press and president is marked by "cooperation and continuity" as well as conflict.[43] The press often finds it necessary to oppose government officials, because it does not feel that the information made available to it is sufficient for newspaper readers to base their decisions on:

Although the press affords the bureaucracy ready access for communication to the citizen, it also operates in another capacity. Messages of governmental publicity do not necessarily fulfill all the informational requirements of the citizen participating in the opinion process. It is a primary function of the news media to obtain such additional information as is required to fulfill these needs.[44]

At the same time, the press finds itself criticizing governmental actions. This happens in part because its notions of objectivity lead it to open its news columns to opposing points of view, often by seeking out for comment critics of the policy (thereby giving critics the same status as government officials). It also occurs in part, inconsistently with the notion of objectivity discussed above, because the press feels that there is more to the story or to the decision than governmental leaders are making known. Dunn said, "Reporters think they are responsible for determining the veracity of statements made by public officials."[45]

The point is not that the press feels that public officials are inept or that they are corrupt; rather, it is that the press feels that public officials may do their best but fall short, and that it is the duty of the press to see, as soon as possible, if public officials have failed. William Rivers's justification for the adversary role is worth quoting at length:

The necessity for a challenging journalism does not spring primarily from the fact that officials lie. They do. But far more often, the public is misled because well-meaning, high-minded officials really believe in their policies and programs. They would not be likely to serve well if they did not believe. But believing as devoutly as many of them do, they approach the public interest through a narrow channel and from a narrow perspective. Such men cannot be expected really to *serve* the public interest because their perspectives are so narrow—unless they are called to account by an independent press. The fact that the press has this independent role is part of the genius of the United States Constitution.

These facts have led me to the conclusion that the proper role of the political reporter is that of adversary.[46]

The press thinks of itself as the voice of the people in the councils of government. Grossman and Kumar discovered that some officials shared that view—they quoted Gerald Warren as saying, "On a daily basis, the White House press corps must be assumed to be the people's representatives."[47] It is then incumbent upon journalists to criticize governmental policies if public officials are going to be held accountable to the will of the people. That the will of the people and the will of the press could be inconsistent, reporters prefer not to consider.

Given modern campaign methods, individual voters have little opportunity to pin down a candidate on the specific programs and policies he would adopt if elected. The press has claimed that duty for itself, and the exercise of that duty places the press and candidates in an adversary relationship. Jules Witcover characterized the relationship as "highly charged":

oftentimes tempered by personal cordiality, good will, and good sense on both sides, but always there. Since a political candidate is in the business of putting his best foot forward to get elected, and the press is in the business of holding that foot to the fire, the adversary relationship is inevitable.[48]

Herbert Gans went so far as to suggest that "journalists have begun to take over, from the political parties and from primaries, the task of winnowing the rolls of political candidates."[49] To do so, news people cast themselves in adversarial roles vis-à-vis candidates:

. . . journalists test candidates for their competence to answer critical questions and to avoid making mistakes; their ability to conceptualize . . . issues in a way that will attract an audience; their skill in developing an appealing and consistent public image; and their honesty in dealing with contradictions in their campaigns and their personal lives.[50]

The press can be expected to be as critical of candidates as it is of public officials—the press as critic of government is also the critic of those who would become part of government.

These roles of the press apply most directly to political reporting, and it should be clear that the roles are ideals, not necessarily descriptive of the actual process reporters engage in during their work.

These roles, however, do imply some standards of journalism. As news seekers, reporters choose to communicate some events rather than others; as truth seekers, reporters present their stories in such a way as to facilitate the reader's judgment about the veracity of the statements reported; as critics of government, reporters bring to bear relevant information about policies and programs that government officials may not see fit to make public. More specifically, these press roles suggest some criteria whereby readers may judge whether reporters do an acceptable job in reporting the news.

1. *Accuracy.* Reporters should present facts correctly, report only what is correct, and interpret without distortion when interpretation is called for. Joseph Pulitzer's call for "Accuracy, Accuracy, Accuracy"[51] is not yet out of date. News sources and news readers can expect no less.

2. *Completeness.* Journalists should report what transpires as fully as possible and report statements edited for space and style considerations but not for substantive reasons. Statements with qualifications attached should be reported with those qualifications, not without them.

3. *Impartiality.* News people should not interject their biases into their reporting and, specifically, should treat statements and appearances by opposing candidates in the same way. This is not to suggest that a false statement may not be challenged, but that a false statement by either candidate should receive the same treatment.

4. *Relevant interpretation.* Reporters should supply background information, supplementary information, and contradictory evidence to the extent the reader needs it to make sense out of the news. The supposition is that particular developments or statements may mean little or may be misleading without a proper context and that news sources may often provide only part of the information necessary to evaluate what has occurred. In the former situation, the news people should provide the requisite context, and in the latter instance, they should add elements the news source did not provide.

These four criteria are similar to several of the criteria used by the New England Daily Newspaper Survey in evaluating press service to communities there. It looked for, among other things, how well the paper covered government at every level; how well the press played its role as a check on government; whether the paper provided a complete and balanced presentation of local, state, national, and international issues; and the paper's integrity.[52] But these criteria are vague. How well is well enough in checking government? Does the evaluation of performance in that role depend on what is happening in the local government at the time? Should a daily newspaper whose circulation overlaps with that of a major metropolitan daily attempt to compete with it in the coverage of national news? How does one determine a paper's integrity?

Although the criteria advanced here are not much clearer if applied to the total news coverage a particular paper may provide, they are useful if one is aware of the source of information available to the reporter when he writes his story. They will be useful in evaluating the treatment accorded the campaign press releases to be examined in this study. Since no newspaper can publish all of the news available to it, it must pick and choose. No two papers are likely to make the same choices, even if they have the identical material available. It would be difficult in that situation to say that one paper, which covered the president's signing of a minor piece of legislation but did not include news of an impending hurricane along the Gulf Coast, provided more complete coverage than did another that used the second but not the first item. Comparing storms with signing bills is difficult. But it is a different matter when the treatment accorded campaign press releases is compared. The question is not then what the priority a story based on a campaign news release might get in one paper but rather whether the paper used the release at all and, if so, in what way. In other words, by applying these standards in this study, I was able to judge whether the press treated the releases accurately and impartially, leaving out no important elements, and provided adequate interpretation, although I was not able to evaluate the total campaign coverage in the press.

Although this study reports the nature and extent of press use of releases in a number of campaigns, the patterns noted are of wider interest. There are many demands for news coverage, some more subtle than others. Editors and reporters recognize immediately that a press release is a request for them to devote newspaper space to the message in the release, but a similar statement made in front of a crowd assembled by an advance person is no less a demand for news coverage. Press releases are less glamorous than media events. They are unlikely to command a front-page headline, but they often find their way into print. They are effective demands for news coverage. The way the press handles this type of demand may be indicative of the way it handles campaign (and political) news in general.

Perhaps more importantly, campaign press releases are communications between candidate and electorate. The information voters need to decide for whom to vote is difficult for them to obtain, and there is no guarantee that campaign releases will provide the facts any particular voter may need to make up his mind. But the functioning of a democratic political system presupposes that voters have access to relevant information about candidates and that candidates have the opportunity to provide that information. Campaign press releases are only one of many means available to candidates to do so, but it is a means that gives them quite a bit of control over the content of the communication. For example, it is more likely that a press release will be run verbatim than a news conference.

The way that reporters treat press releases can influence the effectiveness of releases for candidates and for voters. By providing a relevant context for releases, by inviting opposing comments, and by interpreting the statements made, reporters can make releases a good source of information about campaigns. That possibility, however, depends on what the releases say in the first place.

3

CHARACTERISTICS OF CANDIDATE RELEASES

The first week in October 1973 was a busy campaign week for Charles Sandman and Brendan Byrne, as well as for the reporters covering their activities. Each candidate issued more campaign news releases that week than any other week of the campaign. In a release, Byrne called on the state legislature to "strengthen the state's drug laws" to deal with drug offenders who might try to escape New York's stiffer penalties by moving their operations to New Jersey.[1] In another release, he announced the appointment of Ralph N. Del Deo as state chairman of "Lawyers for Byrne."[2] In a third release, the Byrne campaign reported the endorsement Byrne received from Local 1061 of the Communications Workers of America.[3] That same week, Sandman charged in a release that Byrne was planning to levy a statewide property tax if he were elected governor.[4] Another handout announced the appointment of Arthur Miller as assistant campaign director for the Sandman effort, and a third one accused Byrne of avoiding debates with Sandman.[5] Byrne issued seventeen other releases that week, and Sandman distributed another twenty-two.

This week was not typical. Neither candidate issued this many releases during other weeks, and no other candidates whose releases were examined distributed anywhere close to this number in one week. But this sampling of the Sandman and Byrne releases suggests that campaign releases cover a variety of topics. They range from routine announcements of appointments to minor campaign positions and statements by the candidates on campaign issues to sharp criticism of one another's campaigns. The Byrne and Sandman releases provided a relatively accurate (although incomplete) picture of the campaigns, a conclusion not warranted for releases put out by presidential campaigns, for instance. But reporters who relied primarily on releases for the stories they filed on the Sandman and Byrne campaigns would nevertheless be able to keep their readers current.

In any case, reporters and editors must make two decisions about news releases. First, they must decide whether to use the release at all; second, they must decide how to use the release. In practice, of course, these two questions are interrelated, but since it is possible to think of them as analytically distinct decisions, it is worthwhile to separate the examination of candidate releases into two sections. I assume, for purposes of analysis, that the decision the news person makes about whether to use a release is rapid, given deadline pressures, and must therefore be based on some readily apparent characteristics. The initial decision may be based on factors such as subject matter, length, the number of releases the candidate has recently distributed, and the newsworthiness of the release itself. When the decision to use the release has been made, different criteria become relevant: style, content, and impartial presentation.

The factors of subject, length, rate at which the releases were issued, and newsworthiness are significant when the releases are considered as a whole, rather than one by one. If a campaign is a set of *connected* activities,[6] one would expect releases to be planned rather than random events (although at least one was initially unintended. Herb Wolfe, Byrne's campaign press secretary, said that the Byrne statement on the safety of amusement park rides was released only because it was a slow day).[7] But examining the releases together may reveal patterns that otherwise would escape detection. Similarly, since releases are designed to stimulate news coverage, newsworthiness is relevant. The index developed in this book helps to distinguish those releases with a genuine claim to getting into print from those that have no such claim.

The purpose here is descriptive, and I am not testing hypotheses about the relationship among these factors. Tests of statistical significance, however, are reported when appropriate to strengthen our confidence that the results are not the result of random effects.[8] The characterization of the releases and the differences among the releases of the various candidates serve as the basis for the central hypothesis that later chapters support: that the use of releases by the press reflects both the characteristics of the releases themselves and the difference among the releases of the candidates.

The first step in this study was simply to count the releases.[9] From June 6, 1973, the day after the primary election, to November 5, 1973, the day before the general election, Brendan Byrne's campaign handed out a total of 179 candidate news releases, and Charles Sandman's campaign issued 184.[10] Each candidate averaged a little over one release a day during the campaign. Their totals are virtually the same, which implies that the candidates put a similar absolute emphasis on campaign press releases as a way of communicating with voters (although not necessarily a similar relative—compared to other means of reaching voters—emphasis). Over the period as a whole, neither candidate swamped the news media with releases, but both issued a substantial number.

How substantial is the number they issued can be readily seen by comparing their total with that of other candidates.[11] Mike Antonovich issued a total of sixty-nine releases, counting his primary campaign as well as his general election effort, and Antonovich issued his first release eleven months before the general election. Arlen Specter, running for the U.S. Senate from Pennsylvania in 1980, issued sixty-two issue-oriented releases covering both the primary and general election campaigns. Wendell Bailey, a congressional candidate from Missouri in 1980, and Jim Inhofe, running for Congress from Oklahoma in 1976, issued fewer: sixty for Bailey for primary and general elections and thirty-eight for Inhofe for the general election alone. Coming close to the rate at which the New Jersey candidates issued releases was the independent presidential candidate in 1980, John Anderson. He distributed forty-nine releases in a little over two months. Such differences no doubt reflect different campaign strategies as well as the specific circumstances surrounding the campaigns.

At the same time, it must be admitted that a number of campaigns issue very few, if any, candidate releases. Three California candidates in the 1980 election, for instance, together sent out a total of five releases. Max Besler, the campaign manager for William Dannemeyer, Republican congressman from southern California, indicated that since they faced only token opposition, they issued only one release announcing an upcoming fund raiser. The Dannemeyer campaign tried to give the impression that the contest was "a boring race."[12] To the extent they were successful in giving that impression, the opponent would find it that much more difficult to attract media coverage in the highly competitive Los Angeles and Orange County media market. A local incumbent assembly-

man, Ross Johnson of Fullerton, California, issued none—it was unlikely that he could have gained much coverage, given the competition for space.[13] Instead, Johnson relied on direct mail and news-
letters sent to constituents. Philip Anthony, running unsuccessfully
for reelection to the Orange County, California, Board of Supervisors, sent out only four releases, publicizing appointments and
endorsements. His campaign instead involved personal contacts
and precinct walking.[14]

Two Texas incumbent congressmen adopted similar tactics. Ron
Paul, for instance, issued "a maximum of only 5 or 6 press releases"
that "centered primarily around the Congressman's campaign
schedule and did not mention the challenger."[15] That kind of strategy makes it more difficult for the challenger to attract media attention. Long-time Austin Congressman J. J. Pickle issued no campaign
releases during his reelection effort. In fact, his district administrative assistant, Reg Todd, indicated that Pickle's office purposely
issued fewer legislative releases during the campaign, to make sure
that editors did not think the candidate was using his office to win
reelection. Pickle "became more selective in what we put out";
some substantive involvement by the congressman became an important criterion.[16] These examples suggest that, although a number
of campaigns do not rely heavily, if at all, on candidate news releases, the decision whether to issue releases is connected closely
to overall campaign strategy.

The second step in this study was to group the releases according
to their subject matter. Many different classification schemes are
possible: by issues, by intended audience, or by originator, for
example. The problem with most such schemes is that it becomes
difficult to compare sets of releases—the candidates may have
addressed themselves to different issues or attempted to reach
different audiences. The classification adopted here leads to work-
able categories, neither too small nor too large, and applicable to
most of the candidates to be considered. The first category includes
campaign statements by the candidate himself. The second is comprised of announcements of appointments to positions in the campaign organization. (If the candidate made the announcement of
the appointment, the release is still classified as an appointment
release rather than as a candidate statement.) A third category reports the endorsements the candidates received. The last two categories differ from the first in that they deal with the involvement

of other people in the candidate's campaign; they differ from each other in the kind of involvement. The fourth category includes miscellaneous releases, many of which are statements by persons other than the candidate, announcements of future events, and human-interest stories.

Table 3.1:   Number of Candidate News Releases by Candidate and Category

CANDIDATE[a]	CATEGORY				
	Candidate Statements	Campaign Appointments	Endorsements	Miscel-laneous	TOTAL
Brendan Byrne	53	52	48	26	179
Charles Sandman	70	57	15	42	184
Pat Roberts	17	0	5	4	26
John Anderson	24	7	1	17	49
James Inhofe	30	0	2	6	38
David Boren	30	0	2	10	42
Michael Antonovich	32	14	17	6	69
Wendell Bailey	10	1	22	27	60
Arlen Specter	61	0	0	1	62

Source: Compiled from information supplied by candidates or their campaign staffs.
a. Only candidates for whom at least twenty-five releases were available are included.

Table 3.1 shows how the candidates' releases were distributed among these four categories. Byrne's releases were mostly divided among the first three, and Sandman's releases fell predominantly into the first two categories. In contrast to Byrne, Sandman had only fifteen endorsements to announce, although Sandman would dearly have loved to issue more. But he simply did not get as many endorsements during the campaign as Byrne. That more of Sandman's releases were candidate statements than Byrne's may be explained by noting that Byrne had a greater number of supporters of stature who were willing and able to speak for him—Sandman did not command such support, even among Republicans. Anderson's releases were evenly split between candidate statements and miscellaneous releases. The miscellaneous releases, by the way, told much of the story of the campaign's attempt to get Anderson's name on the ballot of all fifty states. Other noteworthy distributions of releases among the categories involve Bailey and Antonovich. Bailey issued very few candidate statements but had a greater proportion of endorsement releases than any other candidate listed. Antonovich came closest to the pattern of the Byrne and Sandman campaigns, with substantial numbers of releases in the first three categories.

An interesting difference between Byrne and Sandman appears when campaign appointment releases are broken down into statewide campaign appointments and appointments to local campaign organizations. Although each candidate made numerous appointments in both categories (as would be expected), Byrne made considerably more to statewide positions, and Sandman's appointments were relatively evenly balanced between the two. It appears that Byrne needed to appoint fewer persons to local campaign positions, because he found it possible to work with and through existing local party organizations. Sandman, on the other hand, had fought the Republican local organizations in the primary and had not succeeded in reconciling the liberal wing of the state Republican party to his candidacy. It was therefore necessary to bypass the local units and replace them with organizations loyal to Sandman.

There are some noteworthy differences among the candidates in the length of their releases (table 3.2). Although campaign advisors such as James Brown and Philip Seib suggested that press releases "should be as brief as possible," and although editors seem to prefer shorter releases, candidates do not follow such advice consistently.[17] Some advantage can be gained, however, by issuing short releases. Michael Grossman and Martha Kumar pointed out that the White House frequently issues short televised statements, because longer statements would have to be cut to fit the network newscasts. "The implication is that by giving a short statement, the White House is more likely to get what it wants on the news than it would be if editors decided what portion of a longer speech to use."[18] A parallel argument can be made about campaign news releases.

Nevertheless, many candidates often issued lengthy as well as short releases. The longest Byrne release, for example, was eleven times longer than his shortest release, and the longest Sandman release was more than sixteen times longer than his shortest. The

Table 3.2:   Average Length of Candidate News Releases by Candidate and Category (in Lines)

CANDIDATE[a]	CATEGORY				
	Candidate Statements	Campaign Appointments	Endorsements	Miscellaneous	AVERAGE LENGTH
Brendan Byrne	33.3	19.7	18.5	28.5	24.7
Charles Sandman	34.2	19.9	36.4	30.0	29.0
Pat Roberts	29.1	—	17.3	19.8	25.5
John Anderson	26.0	22.6	21.0	26.7	25.7
James Inhofe	21.6	—	28.0	10.8	20.3
David Boren	29.2	—	21.0	22.5	27.0
Michael Antonovich	34.4	33.1	21.5	24.8	30.3
Wendell Bailey	20.2	18.0	14.3	8.8	13.0
Arlen Specter	45.7	—	—	19.0	45.3

Source: Compiled from releases supplied by candidates or their campaign staffs.
a. Only candidates for whom at least twenty-five releases were available are included.

data that follow are based on the estimated length of each release, standardized to a seventy-space pica line. Lines ending short of midpage were not counted; longer lines were counted as full lines.

Sandman was more verbose than Byrne, as far as press release linage is concerned. His 184 releases contained a total of 5,334 lines, for an average of 29.0 lines per release. His Democratic opponent had only a total of 4,419 lines in his releases, for an average of 24.7, more than four lines per release less than Sandman. This difference of 20.7 percent in total linage would not warrant much attention, given the rather crude measure used to derive the figure, were it not that the difference between the two candidates was so consistent. The standard deviation for the length of Sandman's releases was 16.7 lines, and the comparable measure of Byrne was 12.3 lines. Not only were Byrne's releases shorter on average, but his releases were clustered more closely together (in length) than were Sandman's. Sandman's releases were much more varied in length.

Neither candidate issued releases as long as those of Arlen Specter, whose releases averaged 45.37 lines. The selection of Specter's releases available to me, however, were comprised almost exclusively of candidate statements, which tend to be longer than other categories of releases. Still, Specter's releases were quite a bit longer than Sandman's in the candidate-statement category (34.2 lines). Congressman Floyd Fithian of Indiana, who issued only five releases during his 1980 general election campaign, averaged releases of 33.0 lines. Most of the other candidates kept the length of their releases in the range of about 20.0 to 30.0 lines or shorter.

One candidate had consistently short releases: Wendell Bailey, running for Congress from Missouri's Eighth District in 1980. His sixty releases from both the primary and general election campaigns averaged only 12.95 lines; no other candidate had releases consistently that short. Fithian averaged 24.3 lines, in only nine primary and general election releases, since he stressed different means of reaching voters, principally a series of town meetings. James Inhofe of Oklahoma issued thirty-eight releases that averaged 20.26 lines, but that is still substantially above Bailey's average. The brevity of Bailey's releases can probably best be accounted for by referring to the type of campaign he ran: a friends-and-neighbors campaign. Bailey did not go out of the way to raise issues, and most of his releases fell into the endorsement (twenty-two of them) and the miscellaneous (twenty-seven) categories.

In general, the length of the releases in the four categories varied quite a bit among the candidates. The longest candidate statements were Specter's (45.7 lines), and the shortest were Bailey's (20.2 lines). The longest endorsement releases were Sandman's (36.4 lines), and the shortest were Bailey's (14.3 lines). The longest miscellaneous releases were Sandman's (30.0 lines) and Byrne's (28.5 lines). The shortest releases were, once again, Bailey's (8.8 lines). Campaign-appointment releases varied from Antonovich's (33.1 lines) to Bailey's (18.0 lines) followed closely by Sandman's (19.9) and Byrne's (19.7). It is worth noting the large difference between Byrne and Sandman in the average length of their endorsement releases. Sandman's endorsement releases were almost twice as long on average as Byrne's endorsements. The impression one gets is that Sandman's campaign organization sought to emphasize the few endorsements it received by announcing them in longer and (they hoped) more newsworthy press releases.

The releases, then, are different in length and in their distribution among the categories of releases, and they vary tremendously in the number the candidates issue. There would be little more to say about the readily apparent features of releases to which reporters could be expected to respond quickly, if all of the releases were sent to the newspapers on the same day. But, of course, that is not so. A campaign is a series of connected activities, and the rate at which releases are sent to newspapers and the timing of their distribution are important parts of campaign strategy. What is important is the *flow* of releases from candidates to the press.

I am concerned here with the patterns of releases from these candidates. To conduct this part of the analysis, I divided the campaign into weeks, using a Sunday-to-Saturday division. Since the number of releases issued on specific days varied a great deal, with many issued on some days and none or only a few the day after, treating releases by week of issue instead of day of issue smooths out the pattern. Furthermore, most newspapers are weekly papers; if we think of weeklies as primary recipients of releases, a week-by-week examination makes more sense. In addition, even dailies are on a modified weekly schedule of their own. One need only compare the features carried on different days of the week and the difference in length of the paper on different days of the week of virtually any newspaper in the country to realize that a week-by-week analysis of the flow of releases is appropriate. Accordingly, the releases were placed into weeks. If a release was issued with a time restriction on its use (for example, a release issued September 12 might be marked "for release September 15"), it was placed in the week corresponding to the date when it was available to the press.

Figure 3.1 presents the number of campaign press releases that Byrne issued each week of the general election campaign.[19] Byrne obviously did not space out his releases equally from week to week; in fact, he varied from no releases to as many as twenty releases a week. Mike Antonovich, by contrast, issued an almost constant two releases a week for the last two months of his general election campaign. Pat Roberts (with the exception of one week with two releases and one week with three releases) issued one release a week for the last ten weeks of his general election effort. Byrne seemed to have reached a peak (in the number of releases a week) by the seventeenth week of the campaign (September 30 through October 6, 1973). Arlen Specter, however, reached his peak (ten releases) in the last full week before the election.

There seem to be four distinct periods to Byrne's campaign. The first period extends to approximately the seventh week, basically

FIGURE 3.1: NUMBER OF BYRNE RELEASES BY CAMPAIGN WEEK

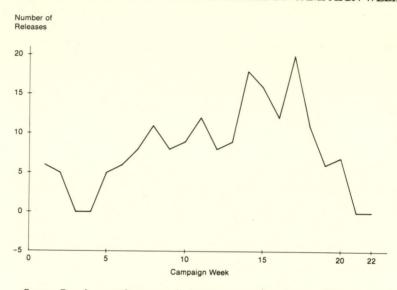

Source: Based upon releases supplied by Governor Byrne's press office.

FIGURE 3.2: NUMBER OF BYRNE RELEASES BY CAMPAIGN WEEK
(Three-Week Moving Average)

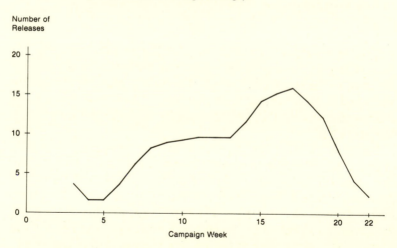

Source: Based upon releases supplied by Governor Byrne's press office.

FIGURE 3.3: NUMBER OF SANDMAN RELEASES BY CAMPAIGN
            WEEK

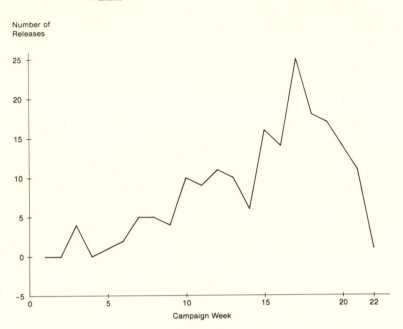

Source: Based upon releases supplied by Representative Sandman's office.

a climb to a plateau. The second period is a plateau extending approximately to the thirteenth week. The third stage is a climb to
the peak in the seventeenth week. The fourth phase is the decline
to the end of the campaign from that point. The three-week moving
average smooths out the curve and plainly shows these four periods.
See figure 3.2.

Sandman's release rate by weeks for the campaign, as shown
in figure 3.3, is similar to Byrne's except for the second stage. The
first stage for Sandman (weeks one through seven) is a climb, but
the second stage does not level off; rather, it seems to climb more
steeply than did the first stage. The third stage, like Byrne's, reaches
the campaign's peak in the seventeenth week by a rapid rise in the
release rate, culminating at twenty-five releases during that week.
The concluding phase is a decline to ground zero. Again, the three-

week moving average for Sandman's release rate confirms the general pattern: a steady rise to a peak, with a sharp decline following. Sandman also did not issue his releases at a constant rate during the campaign and reached his peak at the same time as Byrne. See figure 3.4.

Jim Inhofe's campaign presents an interesting contrast. Inhofe spent about four weeks issuing approximately two releases a week, from late August through late September. At that point, however, he dramatically increased his release rate, issuing nine releases a week on average for the remainder of his campaign. John Anderson, beginning just before Labor Day 1980, issued only one or two releases a week, but starting in mid-September, he began to issue about ten a week. During the last two weeks of his campaign, however, he issued only a total of six releases. Ernie Stromberger reported that the candidate he worked for, John Hill, running for governor of Texas in 1978, issued three releases a day, one at each of the three television markets where the candidate appeared each day (and allowing the wire service to distribute the information to other papers).[20] But the patterns produced by Byrne and Sandman were not duplicated by the other candidates examined here.

That is not to say that some substantial differences between the rates at which Byrne and Sandman issued releases did not exist. Quite the contrary. Byrne consistently issued more releases than did Sandman for most of the first part of the campaign. Not until the sixteenth week did Sandman consistently issue more releases than Byrne. After nine weeks, Byrne had already issued forty-nine releases, but Sandman had issued only twenty-one. The difference can simply be accounted for in the different strategies their campaigns adopted. Byrne found it necessary to keep his name in the press as much as possible, because he could not count on most voters knowing his name.[21] Sandman, on the other hand, planned a late blitz, devoting most of the summer to planning, preparing, and building his organization. His campaign was not as active during that period, and the result was fewer releases.

But at the end of the campaign Sandman issued many more releases than did Byrne. During the last six weeks of the campaign, Sandman distributed almost twice as many releases as Byrne, eighty-six to forty-four. There were two reasons for this difference, both related to the success of the Sandman campaign, or lack of it. For one thing, Sandman had been having difficulty raising money to

FIGURE 3.4: NUMBER OF SANDMAN RELEASES BY CAMPAIGN
WEEK (Three-Week Moving Average)

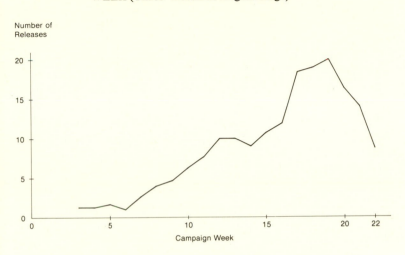

Number of
Releases

Campaign Week

Source: Based upon releases supplied by Representative Sandman's office.

pay for television time; he therefore had to rely more than he had
planned on exposure in the press.[22] Byrne, however, had no such
problems and could begin to concentrate more of his resources on
television in those last weeks. In addition, Sandman had fallen quite
a distance behind in public opinion polls.[23] It is reasonable for a
candidate in such a position to try everything possible to win. Given
the fact that Sandman was short of money and already had a full
personal-appearance schedule (as do all candidates late in a campaign), it was reasonable to increase the number of releases issued.

The upshot was that Sandman did not start to catch up in the
number of releases made available to the press late in the campaign.
The difference between the release rates can be graphically demonstrated by the difference in the cumulative total of releases each
candidate had issued by the end of each campaign week. Such a
graph is included as figure 3.5. The line represents the total number
of releases that Byrne had issued by the end of each week of the
campaign minus the total Sandman had issued. It is, in other words,
a demonstration of Byrne's edge in the number of releases already
sent to the press since the start of the campaign. It confirms the

FIGURE 3.5: BYRNE CUMULATIVE RELEASE TOTAL
                MINUS SANDMAN CUMULATIVE RELEASE TOTAL

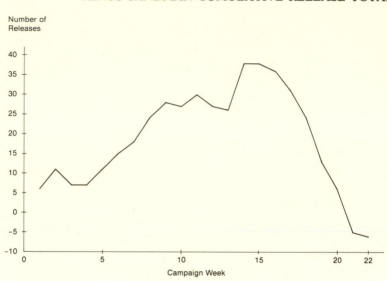

Source: Based upon releases supplied by Governor Byrne's press office and Representative Sandman's office.

conclusions already reached. Byrne steadily increased his edge over Sandman during the first third of the campaign and maintained that lead (and even increased it somewhat) until the end of September. Then Sandman's concentrated flurry of releases, combined with a reduced release rate for Byrne, overcame Byrne's lead, but it was not until the twenty-first week of the campaign that Sandman passed Byrne. Up to that point, New Jersey newspapers had received more releases from Byrne than from Sandman. One would expect that the press would use more Byrne releases during most of the campaign. Chapter 6 confirms this expectation.

Reporters who may use campaign releases, however, are unlikely to think of releases in terms of such patterns, although they may sense some characteristics of the release rate. They are more concerned with other factors: the subject of the release, its length, and its newsworthiness. Newsworthiness is an elusive concept that I tried to pin down in chapter 2. There I listed five characteristics of a newsworthy development. Such an event had recently occurred, it involved conflict, it had significant impact, it was un-expected, and it involved noteworthy people. It is to be expected that if reporters use these characteristics as criteria to determine whether to file a story on a development, they will use the same criteria in determining whether to use a campaign press release. Reporters must make decisions about using releases quickly, and so newsworthiness is an appropriate characteristic of releases to consider in this chapter. Since it is reasonable to expect campaign news releases to differ in their newsworthiness, it is also reasonable to compare them on that score.

I have constructed a newsworthiness index that incorporates these five characteristics of a newsworthy occurrence. Points are awarded the releases depending on the presence of these factors, and the total represents how newsworthy the release is. The first criterion is timeliness—releases indicating that a recent develop-ment is being reported have a better chance of being used. Two points are awarded if the release reports an event that took place "today" or "yesterday." One point is given if the release indicates that the event took place "this week," but no points are given if the release does not indicate when the event took place.

The second criterion is the presence of conflict. Since these are campaign releases, the conflict that is most relevant is conflict with the opponent. Therefore, two points are awarded if the candidate or other person disagrees with or criticizes the opposing candidate or campaigners. One point is given if the release reported a criti-cism of a third party, one not connected with the opposing party No points are awarded if there was no conflict apparent in the release.

The third criterion is the impact of the event reported. Two points are awarded if the development has significant potential impact and that impact is likely to be felt over a large area—more papers would have a reason to use such a release. One point is given if the significant potential impact is local. No points are awarded if there is likely to be little, if any, impact from the event reported.

The fourth criterion is unexpectedness. There are two possibilities here. Either the development in the release was unexpected, in which case a point is awarded, or it is not, in which case no points are given.

The fifth criterion is the VIP factor; developments involving important persons are more newsworthy. Two points are given a release if the candidate or other noteworthy person, such as a statewide officeholder or a national political figure, is either the source of the news or is quoted in the release. However, candidates for local office are not as newsworthy, and for their participation, only one point is awarded. One point is awarded also if another prominent person, such as a campaign manager for a major campaign or a well-known state legislator, is the source of the news or is quoted in the release. No points are awarded if the campaign in general is the source of the release.

In effect, when the scores of the releases on each of the components are added, the impact of each factor is weighed equally with that of the others, with the exception of the unexpectedness component, which contributes one point at maximum. Few releases, however, report unexpected developments. When they do, unexpectedness is an important factor, as the weight given the factor in the regression reported in chapter 6 indicates. Overall, this index evaluates the newsworthiness of releases conservatively. To the extent that it estimates inaccurately, it tends to understate the newsworthiness of candidate releases.

This index varies from nine points for the most newsworthy releases to zero points for the least newsworthy. A release that would receive the maximum score on this index would be one that reports a very recent event where one candidate criticizes the other on an unexpected matter with statewide impact. It is reasonable to expect few such releases. Candidates are likely to exploit such newsworthy situations in different ways, by holding a press conference, for example, or by doing something to catch the attention of television news people. Arnold Steinberg commented, "The more newsworthy the campaign activity, the less likely that a simple news release will be sufficient."[24] (Releases may, however, be handed out during press conferences as well, but candidates would rarely use a release alone to handle a newsworthy situation.) Most releases, in other words, are likely to report relatively routine matters, matters that may be important enough to warrant press attention, but not important enough to warrant much personal involvement by the candidate.

The expectation that releases in general are not very newsworthy is borne out by the average newsworthiness score. That average, for the over 750 releases examined, was 3.54. Brendan Byrne's releases, taken separately, averaged 3.69 on this index, and Charles Sandman's average score was 3.59, an inconsequential difference.

Only 1 release, by Brendan Byrne, was awarded the maximum score, and 9 others, 6 from Sandman, 2 from Byrne, and 1 from John Anderson, scored 8.0 points. On the other hand, 55 releases were awarded no points, and another 53 merited only 1.0 point. By these criteria, then, some releases were not worth the effort, but some were quite newsworthy. See table 3.3.

A look at some releases that score highly on this index and some that score poorly illustrates the difference between them. The release that got the maximum score was issued on October 5, 1973, for press use on October 7.[25] In this release, Byrne criticized Sandman directly and vigorously on Sandman's proposal to have the federal government assume welfare costs, which Sandman said would require a 10 percent surtax on the federal income tax to be adopted. The release was newsworthy not only because it was timely or because it quoted Byrne, but because the issue had significant potential statewide impact, because the candidate criticized his opponent, and because releases in which Byrne directly criticized Sandman were rare and therefore unexpected. But the Byrne release issued October 22 of that year had little news value at all.[26] It rated no points, because it merely announced the endorsement of Byrne by a

Table 3.3: Distribution of Candidate News Releases by Newsworthiness

NEWSWORTHINESS	ABSOLUTE FREQUENCY	FREQUENCY (PERCENT)	CUMULATIVE FREQUENCY (PERCENT)
0	55	7.3	7.3
1	53	7.0	14.3
2	155	20.5	34.8
3	64	8.5	43.3
4	209	27.6	70.9
5	83	11.0	81.9
6	102	13.5	95.4
7	25	3.3	98.7
8	9	1.2	99.9
9	1	0.1	100.0
Total	756	100.0	

Source: Computed from releases supplied by candidates or their campaign staffs.

small union local. There was no indication that the endorsement had just recently been decided, there was no criticism of Sandman, no important issues were raised, and there was no quotation from any prominent person. By the end of the campaign, a union endorsement for Byrne was hardly unexpected.

One of the releases that received eight points on the index reported Sandman's determination to make the potential state income tax the dominent issue in the closing days of the campaign.[27] This release rated a high score on four of the five criteria in the index, but it was awarded no points on the unexpectedness factor, because Sandman had commented on the income tax issue so often by the end of the campaign that yet another release on the subject was no surprise. But the potential impact of the issue was significant and certainly would affect the entire state. The release reported a timely statement, it quoted Sandman directly, and it was critical of Byrne. The Sandman release that announced the appointment of the chairman of the absentee ballot drive in nursing homes was not, however, newsworthy on any of the five criteria used in the index.[28] One can hardly call such an insignificant appointment unexpected, the release gave no indication when the appointment had actually been made, it had little if any potential impact, and no prominent person was involved in the announcement. In addition, there was no criticism of the Byrne campaign in the release (and as a matter of fact, no praise for the Sandman effort, either).

If the newsworthiness index is divided into three groups, low newsworthiness (scores of zero to two), medium newsworthiness (three to five), and high newsworthiness (six and above), some striking differences among the candidates emerge. Over 80.0 percent of Bailey's releases, for instance, fall into the low category, and only two out of his sixty releases rated six or above on the index. Jim Inhofe, on the other hand, issued twenty-three releases that ranked high in newsworthiness, over 60.0 percent of his total. Mike Antonovich had no releases that scored high on this index; his releases were divided fairly evenly between low (44.9 percent) and medium (55.1 percent) newsworthiness. Interestingly, John Anderson's forty-nine releases were divided as evenly as they could be, with sixteen in the lowest and highest categories and seventeen in the medium grouping. In comparison to these disparities, differences between Byrne and Sandman were slight. Sandman's releases were more likely than Byrne's to fall into the medium category. But the greatest difference here was less than 12.0 percent. See table 3.4.

Table 3.4: Distribution of Candidate News Releases by Newsworthiness Category and Candidate

CANDIDATE[a]	NEWSWORTHINESS CATEGORY			
	Low (0-2)	Medium (3-5)	High (6-9)	TOTAL
Brendan Byrne	57 (31.8%)	92 (51.4%)	30 (16.8%)	179
Charles Sandman	70 (38.0%)	73 (39.7%)	41 (22.3%)	184
Pat Roberts	11 (42.3%)	14 (53.8%)	1 (3.8%)	26
John Anderson	16 (32.7%)	17 (34.7%)	16 (32.7%)	49
James Inhofe	5 (13.2%)	10 (26.3%)	23 (60.5%)	38
David Boren	17 (40.5%)	24 (57.1%)	1 (2.4%)	42
Michael Antonovich	31 (44.9%)	38 (55.1%)	0 (0.0%)	69
Wendell Bailey	50 (83.3%)	8 (13.3%)	2 (3.3%)	60
Arlen Specter	0 (0.0%)	55 (88.7%)	7 (11.3%)	62

Source: Computed from releases supplied by candidates or their campaign staffs.
a. Only candidates for whom at least twenty-five releases were available are included.

There may be some relationship between newsworthiness and length. Sandman's endorsement releases, for example, are somewhat more newsworthy than Byrne's, and they averaged quite a few lines more. Cross-tabulating the newsworthiness categories used above with given categories of release length (with cutting points chosen so that approximately 20 percent of the releases fall into each group) indicates that there is such a relationship. Cramer's V is a moderate .307, and the result is statistically significant at the .0001 level. Computing a correlation between newsworthiness and release length supports this conclusion: the value for r is .365.

Actually, the corresponding correlation coefficients for the Byrne and Sandman releases taken separately are somewhat higher. Byrne's coefficient was a substantial .461, and the Sandman figure was .386. The two variables, then, seem to be related, but length accounts for only 13 percent of the variation in newsworthiness. See table 3.5.

The reason for the relationship is not difficult to infer. It is possible that longer releases simply give release writers more opportunity to include the elements the index uses. It is more likely, however, that more important developments receive more detailed and therefore longer treatments in the releases. Although there are exceptions, releases that announce newsworthy events or statements tend to be longer than other releases.

It is likely that reporters can determine quickly how important a particular release is. It is likely, too, that the elements of the newsworthiness index we have developed here are the ones that will catch reporters' attention. There should be, then, a correlation between newsworthiness and use of releases by the press. The higher the newsworthiness score, the more likely it should be that the press will use a release, and the more likely it will be that more than one paper will use it. This is one of the main hypotheses that later chapters test.

Reporters respond first to the readily apparent features of releases. It is that first response that will weigh heavily in their decision to use or not to use a particular candidate news release. Which candidate issued it is one such feature. Whether reporters are indifferent

Table 3.5: Distribution of Candidate News Releases by Newsworthiness and Length

NEWS-WORTHINESS CATEGORY	LENGTH (IN LINES)					
	14 or less	15 to 19	20 to 27	28 to 38	39 or more	TOTAL
Low (0-2)	92	75	53	23	20	263
Medium (3-5)	40	65	73	91	87	356
High (6-9)	9	13	25	45	45	137
Total	141	153	151	159	152	756

Source: Computed from releases supplied by candidates or their campaign staffs.
Note: $X^2 = 142.77$, 8 df, $p < .0001$; Cramer's $V = .307$.

between two candidates is a crucial question that an examination of the use of the Byrne-Sandman release will answer. The subject matter of the releases is also an obvious feature of the releases. Whether reporters are as likely to use statements by the candidates as, for example, endorsement releases is determined in chapter 6. Similarly, when the release is issued is a relevant consideration for reporters. They must take into account how many other releases they have already used. They know, too, that the level of public interest in campaign matters is higher in the fall.

One would expect that the patterns noted here—the distribution of releases among subject categories, the release rates, and so forth— would be preserved by the way in which the press used the releases. In other words, one would expect more Sandman candidate statements to be used than Byrne candidate statements, in part because Sandman issued more. One would expect to see Byrne's edge in issuing releases to be reflected in an edge in press use of releases during the summer. If reporters do make their decisions to use campaign press releases on the basis of the readily apparent characteristics of the release, these patterns should persist.

4

IMAGES AND ISSUES
IN RELEASES

The potential of candidate news releases as devices for communicating with voters is easily underestimated; it would seem not at all likely that conscientious journalists would treat releases favorably. After all, they offer news people "those facts which the press agent *wants* publicized," according to Leo Rosten.[1] But as later chapters demonstrate, campaign releases are widely used, and the beneficiaries are the candidates. David Paletz noted that "mostly mediated messages," which include releases, "can affect the public more than other kinds," because the selective exposure, selective perception, and selective retention mechanisms that guard readers against unwelcome propaganda do not come into play as much "when the candidates do not appear to control the information" voters receive.[2] The potential of campaign releases depends on their publication as news stories. If they are so published, they can be a significant way to communicate with voters.

The success of that method, the impact of the communication, obviously depends on the way in which reporters and editors use releases. The decision to use a release, as noted, was based on the newsperson's response to some readily apparent features of the release. The way in which he decides to use it, however, is based on different criteria. Specifically, the extent to which a release is rewritten depends on how closely the release approaches the type of news story the reporter himself would have written. The release must be accurate, impartial, complete, and provide enough relevant background information to make the news intelligible to the readers. (It must be added that in examining the content closely, editors and reporters may discover that they were wrong in their original decision to use the release, either because it turned out to be less newsworthy than they first thought or because the rewriting required to make the release meet their standards is too extensive.) Candidates would therefore do well to prepare their releases to meet journalistic standards and thereby reduce the probability that the release will be rewritten.

The treatment releases receive determines their potential impact on the electorate; the inconsistency between candidate needs and journalistic standards must not be forgotten. This conflict of criteria is not unique to the relationship between candidates and news people. Roy Carter found a similar inconsistency in outlooks between doctors and reporters who covered medical news.[3] Candidates must take this situation as a given and adapt their releases to it. They must manage to combine their messages to the voters with the format and style journalists will accept. We can expect them to use some devices that meet journalistic standards and at the same time allow them to transmit propaganda past the press watchdogs. The candidates' messages in their campaign releases and the way in which they couched those messages so that the communications could reach the voters are the subjects of this chapter. These devices allow the campaigners to get their messages through.

Here I am concerned with that content, but it is not necessary to use what is now referred to as content analysis.[4] *Content analysis* allows a researcher to make specific statements about the sources he is dealing with by describing their content statistically. Obviously, content analysis refers to examining the content of written materials, but that process in modern guise has become a sophisticated statistical research tool. It is too complex for our purposes, since it requires the construction of a dictionary, a task worth a book in itself, and because I am concerned mainly with the differences between the releases and the news stories—content analysis is not necessary to note such differences.

Although image building is one purpose for campaign messages, the importance of candidates' images may have been overrated in the past. Media consultants do use advertising techniques to "sell" candidates and manipulate their images to evoke desired responses among voters, but these images are the result of more than television spot commercials. Here I simply define an *image* as a set of perceptions an individual has of something or someone else.

These perceptions arise in part from the preconceived notions the individual has (how do you picture a radio personality you have never seen?), including his prejudices and preferences as well as his expectations, and in part from the attributes the object or person being perceived projects. It is possible, then, that different voters would have different images of the candidates, but also that the candidates can influence those images by attempting to project and emphasize attributes they would like voters to perceive and thereby incorporate into their images of them. Although some manipulation of images can occur during campaigns, it takes place within the context of preexisting sets of perceptions voters already have of the candidates. A candidate's image is the result of the information the candidates try to send the voters, the voters' pre-dispositions toward the candidates, their responses to the way he handles himself, and the impressions they get from the way he is reported in the media.

Candidates use press releases as one means of influencing the images voters have of them. Although no candidate has full control over the entire set of perceptions voters may have of him, he can try to emphasize several attributes, hoping that they would form a significant part of the image voters would have of him on election day. At the same time, some candidates also try to stress unfavorable aspects of the opponent's image.

The Byrne releases stressed three attributes: his honesty, experience, and responsiveness to the needs of the people. The Sandman releases stressed two: his experience in government and his consistency on the issues. At the same time, Byrne's releases painted Sandman as too conservative and more interested in the needs of big business than the needs of the people, and Sandman's releases pictured Byrne as politically inexperienced, inconsistent, and too liberal.

Byrne's releases emphasized his honesty and integrity in two ways. He was often referred to as Judge Byrne, thereby clothing him in the prestige of courts, even though he had resigned from the bench to enter the primary. In addition, the releases minimized Byrne's past participation in elective politics, an effective ploy during the scandal-rocked Cahill administration, which had seen the indictment of former Cabinet officials and campaign leaders in Cahill's 1969 campaign. Watergate, too, was beginning to draw more and more attention in the summer of 1973. Political corruption was a dominant theme in newspaper columns. Byrne's image as a man outside politics was an important asset in the primary, and the general election campaign releases used this image to advantage. One Republican who endorsed Byrne said in the release announcing the endorsement, "Judge Byrne has the background and the integrity to return government to its deserved place of respect."[5] Others referred to his "absolute integrity."[6] They called him "an intelligent and honest humanitarian," an accolade any politician might covet.[7]

Byrne's releases stressed his experience, even though he had not participated openly in electoral politics, partially to reduce the contrast between his background and Sandman's legislative experience. In early October, a Communications Workers endorsement referred to Byrne's "experience as a Judge and Prosecutor."[8] A later endorsement from the United Transportation Union referred to Byrne's "record of public service," calling Byrne's performance as President of the New Jersey Board of Public Utilities Commissioners "both memorable and distinguished."[9] Another endorsement stressed both traits, applauding Byrne's "integrity as a public servant."[10]

Public servants, however, need more than integrity and experience; they should be responsive to the needs of the people as well. Such responsiveness was the third characteristic that the Byrne releases regularly claimed for him. As Gene O'Horo, chairman of the Carpenters Non-Partisan Education Committee, said in announcing the committee's endorsement of Byrne:

Brendan Byrne is sensitive to the feelings of the citizens themselves. . . . He knows that a governor has to listen to the people in order to do what is best for the state, and he's ready to represent all of New Jersey.[11]

Henry S. Patterson, a Republican from Princeton, in endorsing Byrne, called him a "capable man who has a feel for people, an understanding of their needs and an awareness of the role government must play in this modern day world."[12]

The Sandman releases, however, provided the same electorate with several good reasons to vote for the Repblican candidate instead. His image was better established with the voters than Byrne's before the 1973 election, but the releases still served to emphasize several attributes involved in that image. Specifically, the releases for Sandman stressed his experience in government and his consistency on the issues. One can depend on Charlie Sandman, the releases said. "At least with Congressman Sandman, . . . we know where we stand. And more importantly, we know where he stands."[13]

His releases made much of the fact that Byrne had never held elective office, and that Sandman had "17 years of service in elected public office."[14] Nelson Rockefeller, then governor of New York, commented on Sandman's "20 years of elected public service at both the State and Federal levels" in endorsing him.[15] "No question about it, . . . Charlie Sandman's long experience in elected offices at both the State and Federal level will be a great benefit to New Jersey during the Sandman Administration."[16] Sandman explicitly contrasted his experience with Byrne's. Byrne's public offices were appointive ones, but Sandman "went directly to the people to be judged in elections," and that experience, according to the releases, would help Sandman become a better governor.[17] Perhaps, Sandman said, Byrne cannot promise that he can run the state without the additional revenue provided by an income tax (and a statewide property tax that Sandman said Byrne wanted to levy[18]), but "I can run this state without either of the big taxes my opponent advocates and without cutting back on programs our people need."[19]

Besides being experienced, according to the releases, Charles Sandman was consistent. "Sandman Opposed Income Tax for 20 Years; Byrne for 20 Days," announced one release headline in capital letters.[20] Sandman often referred to public positions he had taken before. For example, one release noted that "as a State Senator for 10 years and as a Member of Congress for the past seven, Sandman has consistently voted against legislation that required counties and municipalities to spend tax money they didn't have."[21]

Since Sandman took relatively unambiguous positions on some issues (such as unequivocal opposition to forced busing, statewide zoning, and additional state taxes), he was pictured as open. "Sandman speaks plain, his record is open on the tax issue."[22] As long as voters liked the issue positions he took, these attributes would help him develop a favorable image with New Jersey voters.

Other candidates choose similar themes to emphasize in their image-building efforts. Michael Antonovich, who ran successfully for the Fifth District seat on the Los Angeles County Board of Supervisors in 1980, stressed his responsiveness to citizens in a number of his releases. The California attorney general, George Deukmejian, cited Antonovich as "an honest, hard-working legislator who was always responsive to his constituency."[23] The candidate himself, in calling for board meetings in different parts of the county, pointed out that "people in government are always talking about being responsive . . . [but] government can't respond to the people if the people can't get to their governmental representatives."[24] Wendell Bailey, the GOP candidate for Congress from Missouri's Eighth District in 1980, was repeatedly described as just common folk: he is "mainstreet people," with "true down home quality," a man who is "down-to-earth and sincere, yet creative and brilliant."[25]

Opponents often disagreed. Brendan Byrne's releases, for instance, presented a different picture of the Republican candidate. Sandman, too, gave the voters a much different picture of Byrne than they could have gotten from the Byrne releases.

The Byrne releases consistently attempted to portray Sandman as a man isolated from his own party. The United Automobile Workers' endorsement commented on Sandman's "extremist ways."[26] But such a comment from a group unlikely to support a Republican does not have the impact a similar statement from a Republican would have. There was no shortage of such statements from Republicans in the Byrne releases. Leslie Blau noted that "Sandman has consistently adhered to an ideology so conservative that it represents a minority view even within our own party."[27] Lee R. Munsick, described as a conservative Republican, endorsed Byrne, because he feared that "four years with Charles Sandman as Governor of New Jersey would set our state back 20 years."[28]

Ann Klein charged in a Byrne release that Sandman had "consistently adopted to a pro-big business, anti-citizen approach to the vital environmental issues facing New Jersey."[29] This comment typified the notion that the Byrne campaign wanted to spread about Charles Sandman: that he favored big business, which meant that he was opposed to the worker and to the interests of the people. Sandman was blamed for being a "persistent foe of the elderly," for "attempting to deceive the public on the issue of taxes," and for his "general insensitivity to the needs of the people."[30] He was repeatedly pictured as a man who supports special interests at the expense of the public interest: "He has consistently voted with those who would continue to exploit and despoil our environment and against the interests of the residents of the state—and even of his own district."[31]

The Sandman picture of Byrne was likewise uncomplimentary. His releases made much of the fact that Byrne had relatively little experience in public life. Byrne's late entry into the Democratic primary race (announcing his candidacy only days before the filing deadline) made it simple to charge that "Byrne was hand-picked by the Hudson [County] bosses as the Democratic candidate."[32] Byrne's previous offices had all been appointive, which lent credence to the charge that Byrne was boss controlled. Sandman pointed out that "Byrne has never been elected to any office. Every office he has held has been by appointment of a politician."[33] Byrne's position on taxes was attacked via the experience question. His "thinking on fiscal matters shows his lack of knowledge and his inexperience," Sandman said.[34] Byrne was further criticized for his lack of "legislative experience," and he was charged with being "incapable of making the kind of decisions necessary to run a state."[35]

Sandman's releases also stressed what was termed Byrne's inconsistency on major issues. In mid-October, Republicans issued flyers that referred to Byrne as " 'Flipper' because . . . Byrne 'flip-flops' on every issue."[36] The release announcing the brochure contained extended discussions on Byrne's supposed inconsistencies on a state income tax, a state property tax, capital punishment, and abortion. The New Jersey Citizens for Tax Relief called "the Democratic nominee totally evasive" on the tax question, unlike Sandman.[37] In addition, the Sandman releases called Byrne the "candidate of far left politics and radical chic."[38] Citing the notion that "Brendan Byrne has made common cause with the most radical elements in New Jersey state politics," several Democrats, led by Richard Buggelli, decided to endorse Sandman instead.[39] The New Jersey Citizens for Tax Relief, too, decided to support Sandman because "the Byrne camp of liberal fringes continue [sic] to match their fuzzy looks with fuzzy thinking on state finances."[40]

Not all images of opponents presented in campaign press releases are negative; occasionally, the opponent is ignored completely. This tactic is time honored; it is based on the assumption that even negative exposure in the press may be beneficial to the opponent, especially if he would otherwise have difficulty attracting coverage. Pat Roberts, who won the 1980 congressional seat in Kansas's

First District, used this ploy. His Democratic opponent, Phil Martin, was not mentioned at all in the releases. Of course, sometimes it is a better strategy for a candidate to call voters' attention to the less attractive traits of the opponent, especially if the opponent is better known in the first place. Antonovich used this strategy in this campaign, labelling his better-known opponent, incumbent Baxter Ward, "arrogant" and charging that he "has failed to demonstrate effective leadership" in his two terms as County Supervisor.[41] Whether to attack or ignore the opponent is a basic campaign decision, and the releases reflect the strategy chosen.

One important aspect of a candidate's image is the picture voters may develop of them as holders of the office they were seeking. Differences in the images that Sandman and Byrne projected about themselves as governor of New Jersey in the releases concerned an active-passive dimension. Although both candidates took positions that imply they supported governmental action, and both candidates sometimes took a skeptical view of the possibility of effective governmental action, in general, Brendan Byrne's releases pictured him as a governor who would not hesitate to use the authority and instruments of state government to remedy what needs remedying. Charles Sandman's releases showed him likely to be a governor who would keep government out of many social and economic problems, leaving them to be solved by other means. Significantly, the Sandman releases in their image of Byrne as governor supported that very conception of Byrne as an activist governor, and the Byrne releases also showed Sandman as a governor who would be reluctant to use the powers of state government to deal with important state problems.

Byrne's speech before the Democratic State Convention, as reported in a campaign press release, was full of references to possible state actions designed to deal with statewide problems, from a "program to ensure jobs and to protect jobs," to "a state development corporation" to promote development in the central cities, to "planned, orderly development of the state's resources."[42] He later proposed the "formation of a state-wide housing development corporation" and the "enactment of . . . new laws and regulations to protect homeowners."[43] These proposals indicated a willingness to attack widespread problems from Trenton, and a desire to deal with such questions on a statewide rather than local basis. The main attribute the Byrne releases stressed about him as a future governor was activism: Government is a tool that can be used—if there is a need, let us therefore use it.

Sandman's releases presented the same picture, but in a less complimentary light. One release cited a Sandman criticism of Byrne: If Byrne is elected Governor, he'll impose state-wide zoning guidelines and laws," which is quite consistent with Byrne's conception of state government as a tool.[44] He would suggest that if local zoning cannot deal with the problems involved effectively, the state should act. Furthermore, Sandman's repeated assertion that he could run the state without a tax increase, whereas Byrne would require more revenues, was also a hint that Byrne would ask the state to do more, but Sandman could "meet the needs of the state" without raising taxes.[45]

Charles Sandman, however, preferred that the state leave problems to private individuals and to local government to deal with. For one thing, if it was a question of local control versus statewide regulation, the Republican candidate was on the local side: He is a "determined 'home-rule' proponent."[46] In controversies over school busing in North Brunswick, over zoning in Washington Township, or over educational matters, Sandman was on the side of the local officials. For Sandman, the "crucial question remains the same: 'Who rules New Jersey—the people and their elected representatives [meaning local officials] or the judges and the bureaucrats?' "[47] If it was the "meddling of a state agency in the affairs of local communities," which stirred Sandman's anger, one would assume that, as governor, Sandman would therefore not involve the state in questions he considered basically local matters.[48]

The Byrne releases concurred. Edward Manley, in endorsing Byrne, said that Sandman was "unconcerned about the *state's* important responsibility of preparing our children for the future."[49] Others spoke of the possibility that Sandman as governor would "renounce and discard the progressive policies" of the recent past and that he would "bring to a halt years of progress."[50] In effect, these releases suggested that Sandman would end programs "which now receive wide bipartisan support," at least partially because Sandman simply did not think that state government should deal with those matters.[51] The Sandman candidacy was pictured by both Byrne and Sandman as a candidacy that promised a state government that would govern less, rather than more; for the Byrne candidacy, the opposite was true. The releases pointed up, therefore, a significant difference between the two on this important question.

Images, not issues, are the substance of campaign releases, but a large portion of releases are devoted to discussing issues, perhaps out of deference to editors and journalists who seek out "hard news" and new information about candidates' stands on issues. The discussion here concentrates on issues that received quite a bit of space in the releases. The variety of issues raised, of course, is tremendous. Location of airports, tax rates, corruption in government, and defense policies all received some treatment by various candidates. Most of the discussion that follows reports on how Byrne and Sandman dealt with two major issues they both commented on in their releases: tax policies and transportation. I limited myself to examining only those releases that reported statements and positions attributed to the candidates themselves on the assumption that their positions, not someone else's statements about their positions, are central. However, the total campaign discussion on these matters is not reported in the releases, since they do not include candidates' comments at press conferences or their statements at public appearances, nor do these releases reflect the total press coverage these issues received. The discussion in the releases may very well have been different from the discussion in other aspects of the campaign, but probably not greatly different. To determine those differences would require a full-fledged study of its own.

A central issue of the New Jersey campaign was the state's tax policies. New Jersey had long been criticized for having an outdated tax structure, mainly because it did not have an income tax. Because of rising costs and because of the heavy reliance by local governments on the property tax, the property tax was subject to criticism as well. Elderly homeowners as well as those in the market for a new home were concerned with the amount of property taxes they would have to pay. Furthermore, the New Jersey Supreme Court had just ordered, in *Robinson* v. *Cahill,* a change from funding schools through local property taxes, because that system resulted in inequities. Homeowners in areas with high property valuations would be able to provide their school pupils with better facilities and personnel than areas where property valuations were low, even if the actual property tax rate were the same. The opportunity to reform New Jersey's tax policies seemed at hand.

Byrne did not say a great deal about taxes in his releases. He proposed extending the property tax exemption to senior citizens who rented as well as those who owned their homes. Like Sandman, he promised to work for an end to out-of-state taxation (of New Jersey residents who worked in neighboring states and pay income taxes in those states). But about an income tax or a statewide property tax, the releases said nothing. In fact, Byrne did not take a firm stand one way or the other, probably preferring to keep his options open. When the *Robinson* decision was announced, Byrne commented that the "new Legislature [must] not increase the load upon the already overburdened residential real property owner," which left the way open for an income tax as a means to finance public education in the state.[52] But when Governor Cahill said that he expected a $200 million surplus in the budget, Byrne said that the "announcement of the surplus . . . supports what I have said on a number of occasions—that as governor, I would not immediately need a new source of revenue to run the state government."[53]

In his speech to the Democratic State Convention, Byrne spoke of tax policies and said that the court-ordered change in school financing gives the state an opportunity to "redistribute the burden of government," implying a different basis for gathering revenue. At the same time, he listed five criteria that a tax reform package would have to meet:

it must reverse escalating property taxes for the residential taxpayer; it must prevent windfalls for commercial and industrial property owners; it must avoid any increase in the sales tax; it must pay for governmental programs enacted; and it must be capable of generating support in the Legislature.[54]

Few taxes would meet these criteria, but except for doubtful support in the legislature, an income tax would. On June 19, 1973, Byrne said that "the next Governor must take the necessary steps to see that the Legislature complies with the Court's directive [in *Robinson*]."[55] Even from the releases, one can reasonably infer that Byrne wanted to be free to propose an income tax if he thought it necessary after the election.

Charles Sandman's fundamental position on taxes was the status quo. "If you don't want any new taxes," Sandman told the voters just days before the election, "vote for Charles Sandman."[56] The only major change Sandman proposed was property tax relief for senior citizens. Senior citizen property owners would be exempt from paying local property taxes going for education. Otherwise, Sandman's program was critical of Byrne proposals on taxation. Sandman argued that he could run the state without new revenues: "our revenue from all sources, a thumping $3 billion, is sufficient to run the state."[57]

As Sandman saw it, what Byrne wanted to do was levy a state income tax and add a statewide property tax of $2.60 per $100 assessed valuation on top of already existing local property taxes. (Byrne's campaign denied the property-tax proposal, but Sandman claimed that Byrne made the suggestion during an interview with a reporter.) Sandman reiterated his opposition to a state income tax throughout the campaign, an opposition that was spelled out in the GOP platform for 1973. His opposition was based at least partly on the fact that "the people are already overtaxed and overburdened with rising prices. The one thing they can't tolerate is a tax on their hard-earned incomes."[58] Especially in the last two weeks of the campaign, Sandman stressed his conviction that the state did not need an income tax and that it would hit working people the hardest. Add to that Sandman's certainty that the state did not need the additional revenue, and the result is clear: a vote for Sandman was a vote against an income tax.

Small wonder that the man "whose opposition to a New Jersey income tax is legend" reacted to Byrne's failure to rule out categorically the imposition of an income tax.[59] The Democratic party platform for 1973 contained comments similar to those Byrne made during the campaign, calling for tax reform "as a lever to produce a fairer and more equitable distribution of the inevitable tax burden."[60] Sandman referred to that statement as a "deceitfully concealed [sic] hint" that an income tax would inevitably come to New Jersey.[61] Further refusal by Byrne to rule out an income tax unequivocally brought further charges from Sandman that Byrne "refused to make a firm pledge" against an income tax.[62]

Byrne, too, criticized a Sandman tax proposal. Sandman had suggested that the federal government assume the welfare costs normally borne by the states. There was a bill before Congress to do just that: H.R. 1. Sandman anticipated a $100 million savings in existing state funds" from H.R. 1.[63] Unfortunately, it seems Sandman had said that "there will be no H.R. 1 (federal assumption of welfare costs) unless there is a surtax. The two bills are tied together lock, stock, and barrel."[64] That 10 percent federal income tax surcharge enacted to help pay for the Vietnam War was still on the books and up for renewal. Byrne gave H.R. 1 credit for possibly saving the state $250 million, much more than Sandman's estimate, but Byrne suggested that it would cost New Jerseyans $750 million in increased federal income taxes, which, if correct, made H.R. 1 a losing proposition. Byrne challenged "Charles Sandman . . . to explain to the people how that scheme will save them money."[65]

The two candidates also argued about transportation policies, a perennial problem in the major population centers of New Jersey, especially around New York City and Philadelphia. Many New Jersey commuters to New York City use the Port Authority Trans-Hudson railway line (PATH). When the Port Authority proposed raising the fares, both Byrne and Sandman were given the opportunity to take a popular, straightforward position against the fare hike, and both took it. Byrne argued that the Port Authority should subsidize PATH with its "huge operating surplusses [sic] available to them from their tunnels, bridges and the World Trade Center."[66] Increasing the fare will just increase automobile traffic, Byrne said, thereby worsening the air pollution problem in New Jersey. Sandman raised similar objections: the increase would create "more traffic and more pollution."[67] Furthermore, increasing the PATH fare for commuters did not seem fair to the congressman, since the Port Authority "allows a commuter a discount for automobiles using the George Washington bridge and the Lincoln and Holland tunnels."[68] Their positions were no doubt popular with the many New Jersey voters who rode the PATH trains daily.

A second set of transportation proposals, however, provided a contrast. Byrne suggested that the Port Authority be given the primary responsibility to develop "a coordinated transportation system for the port district."[69] Specifically, Byrne proposed "that the Port Authority of New York and New Jersey operate New Jersey's commuter railroads."[70] The reasons Byrne gave referred to the Port Authority's surplus of $80 million and its original mandate "to plan and develop a transportation system for the port district."[71] In other words, Byrne felt that the Port Authority had both the resources and the legal authority to deal with the problem. If an authority such as the Port Authority were given the task of running the bankrupt commuter railroads in New Jersey, these roads would be eligible for substantial federal aid, aid not otherwise available. Covenants in Port Authority bonds that specified the uses of the operating surplus generated by the Authority's tunnels and bridges could be rescinded, Byrne insisted. Operating the New Jersey commuter railroads under Port Authority supervision, supported in part by the federal subsidy and the Port Authority surplus, would make it possible to "solve the transportation crisis this year, not next century."[72]

Sandman vigorously disagreed. He wanted to place the five commuter railroads under a "new transportation authority with far-reaching powers."[73] Creation of a new authority would make New Jersey eligible for the same federal assistance Byrne was counting on. But Sandman argued that "we will not wait for the Port Authority to solve all of New Jersey's mass transportation problems."[74] Sandman's position on the matter was made public just five days after Byrne announced his transportation problem. One month later, Sandman received the endorsement of Philip B. Hoffman, a Port Authority commissioner, who praised Sandman's proposal and criticized Byrne's: Sandman "would call upon the expertise of the Port Authority . . . but would not make the mistake of trying to throw the New Jersey commuter railroad problem into this bi-state agency where 50% of the control lies in New York."[75] Hoffman suggested that if New Jersey asked the Port Authority to assume responsibility for New Jersey's commuter lines, New York would ask for the same thing for its ailing commuter railroads. The "practical effect" would be "no resolution of the problems of transportation in New Jersey."[76] Byrne issued no releases giving his reactions to the Sandman-Hoffman criticisms.

Few candidates issue more than one or two releases discussing their position on any one issue. For instance, Pat Roberts of Kansas put out a release in June of 1980 about water problems, a major concern in his largely agricultural constituency, but he did not find it necessary to add anything to what he said there in succeeding releases.[77] Similarly, John Anderson, in his independent campaign for president in 1980, discussed the role of the "New Right religious groups in politics" in only one release, not mentioning it again, and late in the campaign he called for campaign discussion of the "crisis in the Persian Gulf," a major topic in the media during the campaign but one that none of the candidates broached during their drives for election.[78]

But frequently candidates will issue release after release on basically the same question, merely reworking it from time to time to be able to present it from a new angle. Mike Andrews, running against an incumbent congressman, Ron Paul, in Houston in 1980, repeatedly sought to establish the point that the district's representative should put the district first, and he illustrated that point by calling attention to several votes the incumbent had cast in Congress. A case in point is Andrews's release castigating Paul for voting against a bill designed to deal with oil spills.

It would make more sense for a Congressman from a land-locked state to vote against this bill, . . . but for a Congressman who is supposed to represent a district along the Gulf Coast, where oil production and transportation make waterway spills a particular hazard, such an action is at least very suspect.[79]

Andrews charged that if Paul were reelected, the district would "face two more years of a conservative Republican in Washington who has closed his ears to the cries of the people in this area" while arguing for greater responsiveness to the needs of blacks in the district.[80]

The Republican senatorial candidate from Pennsylvania in 1980, Arlen Specter, frequently issued more than one release on major issues. He stressed the impact of federal policies on Pennsylvania's economy more than any other issue, and he found a surprisingly large number of "pegs" on which to hang the releases. Federal import policies were tied in to Pennsylvania's "struggling apparel industry," to competition from "significant purchases of foreign goods . . . at unfair prices . . . made with federal funds," and the mushroom industry, whose "very survival . . . is currently being threatened by the flood of unreasonably priced canned mushrooms from Taiwan and South Korea on the American market."[81]

The positions the candidates took on issues gave voters some basis for choosing between them. The releases served to help communicate some of the information the electorate needed to decide which one to support. Of course, no candidate tried to present a balanced assessment of the problems facing his constituency. Each stressed the advantages of his proposals and left the disadvantages out of his releases. Reporters and editors no doubt like releases that deal with the issues; they can be expected to consider such releases carefully for possible use. But although some of the releases discussed issues, the candidates were careful to build their images, to stress their favorable attributes (and emphasize their opponent's undesirable traits). In other words, discussing issues was also a means to develop an image, an image that might very well be as decisive as the issues to voters making up their minds.

Few candidates respond very much to their opponents' releases. The instance noted above when Sandman issued his transportation proposals five days after Byrne made his proposals public was one of the few times when the two New Jersey candidates dealt with the same issue from different perspectives within a short period. Even then there was no response by Byrne to Sandman in the releases. This fact is not surprising. LeRoy Ferguson and Ralph Smuckler noticed much the same thing in their study of the 1952 senatorial campaigns:

Analysis of candidate-originated news items and advertisements showed only a few cases where opposing candidates both emphasized the same issues. In the great majority of cases a policy issue emphasized by one candidate received little attention in the press from his opponent.[52]

The point is that although releases served to specify issue positions, they were virtuallly never used to defend a position attacked by the opponent (after all, why publicize an opponent's criticism?). These conclusions support the notion that the purpose of the releases was not to argue for a particular stance beyond announcing a position. Image building is much more likely to be the main purpose of campaign releases.

If this is the essential purpose of releases, to persuade the electorate to think of the candidates in terms of the attributes they stress, it is time to see how candidates wrote their releases to protect this propaganda from elimination by reporters and editors. Blatant propaganda cannot be expected to get past the desk of the local newspaper editor. A release filled with slanted, biased language intended to persuade—propaganda—will most likely not be used, thereby defeating its main purpose—reaching voters. If it is written to meet editorial standards of impartiality and objectivity, it may increase its chances of being used but at the same time jeopardize its other purpose—persuading voters. Sandman, Byrne, and the other candidates whose releases have been examined used four devices to mask their propaganda so that their messages to the voters would survive the editorial process.

Using identifying phrases is a common device. Many of these phrases have already been noted in the discussion of the content of the releases. For example, several Antonovich releases referred to him as "a businessman and former state legislator," stressing thereby both his ties to the conservative business community he was basing his campaign on and his experience in elective office.[83] The advantage of this device is that the main thrust of the sentence is straightforward and objective, diverting the editor's attention from the image building going on at the same time. The release as a whole may report a statement, an appointment, or an endorsement objectively, but the adjectives and adverbial phrases tell a different story. The propaganda is in the description of the candidate and his opponent, not in the report of the event.

Candidates also make use of the fact that public appearances are newsworthy. For instance, both Sandman and Byrne issued releases that reported what the candidate said when he spoke to various gatherings. (Actually, the releases reported what the candidate planned to say, since they had to be prepared before the actual appearance.) A release that calls Sandman "a man who stands far outside the political mainstream" stands a better chance of being used by the press if Byrne actually used those words in addressing the 1973 Democratic State Convention, which he had.[84] Furthermore, newspapers that do not send reporters to cover candidates' public appearances may find a release to be their only source of information about that event. If the appearance itself is newsworthy, these papers may use the release (and the propaganda in it) to provide their readers with coverage.

In his campaign for the Republican presidential nomination, Ronald Reagan used this device differently. His releases almost invariably began, "Governor Ronald Reagan today issued the following statement," followed by the text of his comments on the subject of the day.[85] But his campaign strategy was not oriented toward the print media—it was to get on the nationwide television newscasts every evening. Joel Swerdlow pointed out that "The campaign's virtually exclusive preoccupation with the TV audience made print reporters obsolete—and they knew it."[86] He illustrated colorfully how the presidential campaigns managed to manipulate the media so that they had the opportunity to witness only what the campaign wanted them to see and tried to isolate the reporters so they could not readily validate the independent conclusions they might reach. "Campaign staffs encouraged this, presumably because it increased their control over what reporters wrote."[87] Other candidates, whose campaigns could not control the news coverage nearly so thoroughly and effectively, made extensive use of the device of issuing releases describing public appearances.

Identifying the candidate with specific persons or groups in the releases is another method these candidates used to disguise their propaganda. A candidate endorsed, for example, by the American Conservative Union, is identified with that group in the readers' minds, but a candidate endorsed by the Veterans of Foreign Wars evokes a different image.[88] This technique is valuable, because little editorial rewriting can affect the identification. If a release is newsworthy, it is virtually impossible for the connection between the candidate and the group in an endorsement release not to be reflected in the news story based on the release.

One special kind of group identification must be singled out. Byrne's releases virtually always referred to him as the Democratic gubernatorial candidate, but Sandman's releases referred to his party affiliation much less frequently. When they did so, Sandman's party affiliation was often given in the body of the release rather than in one of the lead paragraphs. Party identification is likely to survive the blue pencil of even the most alert and impartial editors, because editors do not react to party affiliation references as propaganda. In fact, it is to be expected that editors would insert such identification into news stories based on the releases if the releases themselves do not provide it. Paul Weaver argued that objective reporting makes it easy for readers to identify with one side or the other in a conflict because of the tendency to report developments in terms of symbols with which readers can identify.[89] Party identification is such a symbol.

Even though, as John Hohenberg put it, "it is a threadbare device to put a propaganda message in quotes, attributed to a prominent person, in the body of a press release," candidates frequently put hyperbolic statements into quotations in releases.[90] When a prominent person is appointed to a campaign committee the release reporting the appointment often contains a statement by the appointee praising the candidate. Luke Mercadante, appointed to head "Democrats for Carman," the Republican congressional candidate from Long Island, New York, in 1980, said, in the release announcing the appointment:

I have known Greg Carman for many years and have witnessed his work in and with the community. His diligence, intelligence and sympathetic attitude have won my admiration. As a Congressman, he would be visible, available, and helpful. Our district has not had that kind of representation in a long time.[91]

Likewise, endorsement releases give the person or group making the endorsement a chance to explain why this candidate is the greatest thing to come along since whipped cream. Even though these quotations contain blatant propaganda, editors must take it for an objective fact that the words represent his true feelings. Editors can therefore treat the quotation as an objectively correct report of the position taken by the endorser. If the endorsement is news, the reasons for the endorsement are news as well. If the quotation stretches the truth a little, "we would attribute the comments to source of release," said an editor of a large Southern California weekly.[92]

It would be relatively simple for editors to eliminate much of this persuasive content from the releases. Frederik Pohl advised campaigners to expect them to do so, but to hope for the best:

Most newspapermen will cut it [the release] or advise it or even rewrite it and perhaps embody it in a different story of their own; but don't assume that it will happen. Assume that it will be printed exactly as it comes from you.[93]

Ruthless rewriting would reduce quite a few releases into short concise news stories. For instance, the Byrne release announcing the appointment of Fernando L. Santos as state chairman of a "Portuguese Community for Byrne" organization was twenty-nine lines long, but most of it consisted of an exchange of compliments between Byrne and Santos, Byrne citing Santos for his "enormous cultural contribution to the Hispanic community," Santos calling Byrne "one of the most capable men ever to run for governor of New Jersey."[94] An editor will use such a release in its entirety only if his need for material to fill his pages outweighs his negative response to the content, and if he does not have the time to do an effective job of rewriting the release.

That more sophisticated propaganda devices are not used in releases deserves some comment. It is not because campaigners do not have the talent to disguise their propaganda better; after all, they do a good job in doing so with television commercials. Rather, it is because it is not necessary to do so. A surprisingly large number of releases are printed verbatim.[95] Although editors can easily recognize campaign propaganda, their need to fill their news columns, their desire to use material from both candidates, and their wish to provide as much coverage of the campaign as their resources will permit give candidates ample opportunity to get their persuasive messages into the press. Candidates do not have to be very devious.

It would seem, from the relatively straightforward propaganda devices the releases use, that it is easier to get editors to use releases than it is to get television news producers to use staged candidate appearances on newscasts. The reason for that, I presume, is one of supply and demand—there is more space in a newspaper than time on television, and there is likely to be more demand for television coverage. Furthermore, to some extent, the supply of newspaper space is elastic in a sense that time on a television newscast is not. It is easier for a paper to add a page to its next edition than it is for a network newscast to run five minutes longer than scheduled. One might expect that if editors were more hesitant to use releases with obvious propaganda, candidates would become more circumspect in the way they disguise it. Until that happens, however, candidate releases will continue to contain blatant propaganda.

Reporters' examination of releases to determine how they should be used will concern the content, unlike their earlier, preliminary decision to use the releases in the first place. Their close reading of the releases helps them judge the releases by journalistic standards. At the same time, however, reporters will react to more than just a specific release; they are likely to be aware of what the candidates have already tried to present as news. They are likely, as well, to recognize image building in the releases. Furthermore, their own preferences and responses may come into play.

The conflict between journalistic expectations of objectivity and impartiality and candidates' desires to use the press as a channel for conveying slanted, persuasive material to voters would be unimportant if journalists rejected all releases containing any propaganda. Since they do not, their option in treating the releases (printing them verbatim, summarizing them, or rewriting them, for instance) determine whether the candidate will be successful in communicating his propaganda to the voters. The propaganda devices are then crucial for candidates. The task for campaign release writers is to write them to maximize the chances of having the propaganda in the release survive.

5

AMBIVALENT EDITORS' RESPONSES

On October 16, 1973, Charles Sandman announced in a campaign press release his support for a referendum on a bond issue to provide $25 million to construct facilities for severely handicapped children. That day, the Jersey City, New Jersey, *Jersey Journal* reported Sandman's support in one sentence at the end of a longer story about his proposed war on drug pushers; two days later, the *Glen Ridge* (New Jersey) *Paper* published the release in its entirety. Similarly, when Brendan Byrne announced the endorsement he received from the Amalgamated Transit Union, the *Newark* (New Jersey) *Star-Ledger* used several quotations from the release in its story, and the Atlantic City, New Jersey, *Greater Atlantic City Reporter* published the release verbatim eight days later.[1] Editors' judgments about the appropriateness of the releases for their papers are among the reasons for such differences in the way various papers use identical releases.

If there is one generally valid description of editors' responses to campaign press releases in general, it is that they do not seem to like them. Some editors, of course, react favorably to campaign releases, are happy to get them, and are glad to use them, but they are definitely in the minority. The negative responses of most editors to candidate releases, however, seem to be due to the fact that most such releases contain a lot of campaign propaganda and very little news. Of course, the ratio of propaganda to news in releases varies, but the responses of editors to the amount of campaign persuasion in the releases varies as well. For some, the slightest departure from impartial and objective news may be sufficient to reject the release outright.

Their responses to political releases may reflect their evaluations of releases in general. A recent survey reported in the *Wall Street Journal* indicated that business editors "believe that corporate news releases contain irrelevant comments from management and that the important information in the release is buried."[2] Of course, the corporations' purpose in sending out releases is not necessarily to highlight conflict, mistakes, mismanagement, or bad fortune; their purpose is as much to present their enterprises in a favorable light as candidates attempt to project a favorable image. It is no surprise that editors respond similarly to both kinds of releases.

Yet despite the relative distaste editors feel for campaign releases, they do use them. I have become convinced that the ambivalance of editors toward candidate news releases is the result of several factors. First, editors find releases helpful, in providing coverage for the campaign or in steering reporters to a potentially newsworthy story. Second, releases provide quick and inexpensive fillers for their news columns. On the other hand, editors are dissatisfied with the quality of the releases they receive. Facts must be checked out, one-sidedness has to be eliminated, and wording must often be clarified. Furthermore, editors are literally swamped with releases during the heat of the campaign. It becomes more and more time-consuming to sift the chaff from the wheat, and it becomes less and less rewarding as campaigners stress old themes and positions, instead of providing fresh news (even though the old themes and positions may be more helpful to voters). As a result, editors are wary of releases, but they continue to open the envelopes in case the next one is worth the effort.

These comments are impressions only. To be more specific about the responses of editors to campaign releases, this chapter reports the result of three questionnaires on that topic. One survey was conducted in the summer of 1975; a questionnaire was sent to editors of a sample of New Jersey newspapers. A second survey was conducted in the spring of 1976; this time, all editors of newspapers in Nebraska received a questionnaire. The third survey, taken in the summer of 1980, involved a sample of editors nationwide. To a great extent, the earlier two surveys served as pretests for the national questionnaire, but the results are comparable and many of the comments New Jersey and Nebraska editors made on the eaarlier questionnaires were well thought out and aptly phrased. Appendix A reports the data on sampling and return rates. The purpose was to learn about the perceptions editors had about campaign press releases, not to test hypotheses about such perceptions. Whether the insights these questionnaires give are worthwhile depends on how useful they are in interpreting the actual use the press made of the releases they received.

The discussion in the first two chapters of this study suggested that journalists and campaigners are likely to have different standards for judging campaign press releases, and the criteria for newsworthiness, a major component of an acceptable news story, were noted there. It should therefore come as no surprise to find that the editors who responded to these questionnaires often mentioned various elements that comprise newsworthiness. New Jersey editors were asked to specify how they decided whether to use a campaign press release: "It must be newsworthy."[3] "News value. . . ." "Its importance to the public." One editor referred to the conflict between his standards and those of campaigners concisely. He will use a release "if it's newsworthy and not just a partisan statement." A release that makes news is much more likely to be used. As one editor put it, "Too many releases sound like one-sided political bickering."

The specific factor editors mentioned most often was local or subscriber interest. A campaign release tailored to the particular local needs of the editor's paper is most likely to receive a favorable reception. Editors' comments were to the point. They will use a release "if contents affect local area or community; if not, it is discarded." Using the releases depends on their "relevance to our reporting area." Editors nationwide agreed. They were given a list of factors relevant to their decisions to use a given campaign press release, and 155 out of 168 editors checked "local interest." In fact, several editors emphasized that choice by adding stars to it or by ranking the alternatives and giving "local interest" first place.

Of course, what constitutes local interest is by no means clear. It seems likely, however, that editors mean to distinguish between items that relate specifically to their circulation area and items that deal with broader issues that may be significant, but that may be no more important in Poughkeepsie than in Buffalo. This response may be due in part to an attempt to provide a specialized service to the paper's readers, a service other sources of news cannot provide, as well as the desire to avoid competing with larger metropolitan dailies with far superior resources. As one Nebraska editor put it, "Our rule then is this: we let the dailies cover the campaigns, until there is a local tie-in. Then we'll use the information."

Space availability was also a widely mentioned criterion, and deservedly so. When space is at a premium, releases stand less of a chance of getting into print (an important reason why campaigners should see to it that their releases reach the papers with time to spare before the deadline). David Manning White, in his now classic "gatekeeper" study, found that a wire editor was more likely to include stories in his paper early in the evening than later when the deadline was closer:

As the evening progresses the wire editor's pages become more and more filled up. A story that has a good chance of getting on the front page at 7:30-8 o'clock in the evening may not be worth the remaining space at 11 o'clock.[4]

Similarly, Richard Nicolai and Sam Riley found that releases public relations people send to editors have a better chance of being used if they arrive early than if they arrive later.[5]

Three New Jersey editors volunteered the information that space availability was an important consideration. When this factor was included in a list of such factors for Nebraska and nationwide editors, 46 out of 110 Nebraska editors and 59 out of 168 nationwide editors checked it. But it seems that space is more of a consideration for editors of weeklies than it is for editors of dailies. All three of the New Jersey editors mentioning space availability worked on weeklies; 45.7 percent of Nebraska weekly editors cited this factor, compared with only 22.2 percent of the daily editors. The numbers are similar for the national sample: 44.9 percent of weekly but only 24.1 percent of daily editors checked the item. The difference is probably the result of other factors. Dailies, after all, publish between five to seven times a week more often than weeklies and therefore have more space to fill. It seems also, though, that standards for releases are higher for dailies, so daily editors will find space for releases that meet their criteria. Weekly editors, however, with lower standards have more releases that meet those standards on hand, with less space in which to put them. (Information on standards is reported below.)

One factor only a few editors mentioned, but which perhaps many more consider relevant, is whether the candidate advertises in their papers. Editors readily recognize that releases are not really intended to be news stories as much as disguised advertisements for the candidates. The editors who cited advertising as an important consideration feel strongly on the matter. One editor in Nebraska said that his paper never used releases "unless accompanied by advertisement." There are two reasons for such a position. One editor complained, "It's not fair for candidates to pay thousands for spots on TV and radio and expect small business (newspapers like ours) to run their stuff for free! We can hardly afford to stay in business as it is." Besides this economic justification, there is another rationalization:

We also receive very little political advertising from political candidates and we feel if our newspaper is not acceptable as an advertising medium it surely isn't acceptable as a propaganda (which many press releases are) sheet.[6]

It is therefore often worthwhile for a candidate to place a small ad in a paper whose readers he wants to reach. As Arnold Steinberg indicated:

Even modest campaign advertising can be significant for the small weekly. Such advertising may not lead to an endorsement, but it can secure news coverage. In the extreme case, it may be impossible to secure any news coverage without advertising; the implication is that a modest advertisement placed early to show good faith may inspire the editor to use news releases.[7]

There are some differences worth remarking between editors of weeklies and editors of daily newspapers in the factors they consider when deciding whether to use a release. Proportionally, daily editors responding to the national survey were substantially more likely to cite public interest as an important factor. Presumably, public interest in this context means that the editor feels the content of the release deserves disseminaiton, because the public should know the information or because the public would be entertained by it. However, over a third of the weekly editors cited this factor, too, so it is also important to some weekly editors. Editors of dailies were, in addition, somewhat more likely to consider the release's treatment of relevant issues and to look for a controversial position than were editors of weekly newspapers. As already pointed out, space was a more important factor for weekly than for daily editors.

Although "most releases seem to be advertising in disguise," a sizable number of editors say that they use campaign press releases in some way. Of the 157 editors who responded to a question on the first two surveys asking whether they used campaign press releases, only 19 said they never did; only 10 of 168 editors in the national survey said they never did. Very few editors said they used releases "usually" or "always," but given the variety of campaign releases they receive and the uneven quality of some of them, it is not surprising that editors do not say that they rely on releases more heavily. The point is, however, that in most states campaigners have an opportunity to use newspaper columns for their campaign releases.

Weeklies and dailies, however, do not seem to be equally receptive to campaign news releases, although the responses point in different directions. Nationally, daily editors seemed to be more likely to use campaign press releases than weekly editors, but the relationship is weak (Cramer's V = .221), and it is not statistically significant ($p < .15$). The two earlier surveys, however, uncovered a weak relationship (.194) in the other direction, significant at the .05 level, when the results from the two states were combined. But weeklies rely on campaign press releases for a much greater proportion of their campaign coverage than do dailies. The relationship is moderate (Cramer's V = .319), and it is statistically significant at the .01 level. No doubt dailies in general cover politics and campaigns in more detail and therefore have more opportunity than weeklies to use releases. But since they tend to cultivate more news sources than most weekly reporting staffs do, their reliance on releases for campaign news is proportionally lower.

There is, additionally, another use editors make of campaign press releases. Quite a few Nebraska editors volunteered the information that releases are valuable for editorial background, for familiarizing the staff with a candidate and his positions, even if the paper never uses the releases in a recognizable format. One editor went into some detail on such uses:

We . . . use issue-oriented releases as background material, at times to give us questions to raise at press conferences or in questionnaires [to] candidates, also in summarizing their positions, and occasionally to develop articles in which we might contact rival candidates about allegations being made.[8]

Another indicated that he filed the releases he received as "background information . . . for future reference." It can be to the advantage of the candidate to have editors use his releases in that way, because it may lead to a more positive impression of his candidacy: Here is a man who made his positions known. Unfortunately, there is another side to the matter, as there is in so many instances. There is no guarantee that editors will respond favorably even to releases they use only for background: "For one thing," a Nebraska editor pointed out, "sometimes the press releases offer fodder for the editorial writer; especially if the editorial policy of the newspaper differs from that of the candidate."

It is hard to say whether on balance the use of releases for background helps or hurts the candidate. Only about 40 percent of editors responding to the national survey indicated that they used releases for editorial background information; for the other 60 percent, presumably, the candidate's campaign would be unaffected. Also, the net result of a negative editorial developed from press releases may still be politically valuable to the candidate—it results in increased name familiarity, perhaps, or stimulates greater awareness of the fact that the candidate is raising issues in his race. Howard Hunter, the Oklahoma GOP chairman, indicated that the risk of having releases used as a basis for unfriendly editorials was well worth the benefits derived from sending releases out.[9] The problem is greatest with daily papers, however, since results from the national survey indicate that daily editors are more likely than weekly editors to use releases for editorial information.

Editors use releases despite the negative responses most of them have toward the handouts. To gauge the extent of those negative responses, editors were asked whether most campaign press releases require rewriting. Of course, the more editors think releases require rewriting and the more rewriting they actually do when they use the releases, the less likely it will be that the candidates' messages will reach the voters. Overall, the results are clear: only ten editors nationwide said that releases "never" or "seldom" require rewriting, and 129 said they "always" or "usually" called for that treatment. The negative response is clear, but it is not evenly distributed between editors of weekly and of daily newspapers.

Daily editors are more likely to call for rewriting than their counterparts on weekly newspapers. Cramer's V is a moderate .306, and the relationship is statistically significant at $p < .01$. See table 5.1.

Comparisons of the use of releases by papers of different sizes do not lead to clear conclusions. One might expect that smaller weeklies, with fewer resources of their own to use in covering campaigns, would rely more heavily on candidate releases than larger weekly papers. That does indeed seem to be the case. Editors of smaller weeklies say that a greater percentage of their campaign coverage is generated by campaign press releases (Cramer's $V =$ .368, $p < .06$). But the level of statistical significance is not reassuring, based as it is on eighty-nine responses to the national survey. What may be a large weekly by the standards of some states may be a small weekly by the standards of other states. Dividing the responding papers into two circulation groups may not, then, actually lead to putting similar papers together and separating dissimilar ones. Using two circulation categories for daily papers leads to a smaller coefficient of association (Cramer's $V = .224$), but one that is not close to statistical significance ($p < .38$).

In fact, editors of smaller papers did not differ in important respects from their colleagues on larger papers on any of the responses with the exception of daily editors' responses on the need to rewrite campaign press releases. Here editors of larger papers indicated forcefully that releases "usually" or "always" needed to be rewritten (96 percent of all responses fell into these two categories), but editors of smaller dailies (who nevertheless were still likely to call for rewriting of releases) were less critical of releases. Papers that publish more frequently and that reach more readers guard their news columns more diligently.

One inference to be drawn from the fact that most editors think campaign press releases need rewriting before they can be used in their papers is that releases can be materially improved. An open-ended question on all three questionnaires served to elicit some suggestions from editors for improving releases. Editors' responses to this question were far ranging, with as many as five Nebraska editors suggesting that releases not be sent at all: "The best 'press release' is for the candidate to meet the press." Two Iowa editors suggested that candidates send out "fewer, but better" releases. A Wisconsin editor bluntly suggested, "Don't send so many that it becomes almost automatic to deposit them 'in the round file.' "

Table 5.1: Rate at which Editors Say Candidate News Releases Need Rewriting by Type of Newspaper

| | **FREQUENCY** | | | | | |
	Never	**Seldom**	**Occasionally**	**Usually**	**Always**	**TOTAL**
Daily editors	0 (0.0%)	3 (3.9%)	4 (5.2%)	26 (33.8%)	44 (57.1%)	77 (100%)
Weekly editors	1 (1.1%)	6 (7.0%)	20 (23.3%)	30 (34.9%)	29 (33.7%)	86 (100%)
Total	1	9	24	56	73	163

Source: Computed from questionnaire responses, 1981.
Note: $X^2 = 15.69$, 4 dr, $p < .01$; Cramer's $V = .306$.

Other suggestions were more helpful. Many editors insisted that releases were simply too long, that they should be cut, and cut to the bone. "Make them shorter—include only relevant information" was a typical answer. One editor is worth quoting at length on this subject:

Make them shorter. Most releases I received were announcing a candidacy and they would include a biography, views, big issues, experience, and why the candidate is running. The releases would make a story usually between 15 & 20 inches.

Unfortunately most people I've talked to can't stand political news and they won't even start that long of story [*sic*]. But a two to five inch story is read by about everyone, even if it is about the price of peas in Nepal.

Candidates can't expect editors to apportion their releases to readable sizes. I love political news, but I don't. When I have time or the need to dig for news I look for local names and situations. Also the immediacy of the daily mail and daily happenings keeps me from digging in my files for news. And I like to keep a neat desk.

So I'm saying releases should cover one specific topic, be concise and timely. Not only would they be more readable but it would keep the candidate's name in the news more than a one-shot-cover-everything release. They would have to send out more releases and it would cost their campaign more. But they would get much better press.[10]

It seems editors think campaign release writers write as if they are paid by the word. One Pennsylvania editor thinks "They grind them out in public relations offices apparently in justification of their salaries—ghost written for the politician." For editors, brevity may be more than the soul of wit; it may also be the key to getting a release into print.

Another frequent suggestion editors have for improving campaign releases is that writers adapt them for the local circulation areas of the papers to which they are sent. The justification for this suggestion is clear: what is likely to be of interest to a paper's readers is likely to concern them. Over 92 percent of the editors responding to the national survey checked "local interest" as one of the most important factors in deciding whether to use a particular campaign press release. One New Jersey editor said, "We tailor coverage to our area. . . . Only if the news content in the release is helpful to our readers, in our opinion, would we consider releases." As a Nebraska editor described it, newspapers are analogous to politicians:

A newspaper, like a candidate, has a constituancy [*sic*]. My constituancy [*sic*] does not want to hear about New York, or even about Omaha and Lincoln.

They want, as far as politics goes, something relating to *their* role, *their* responsibilities, *their* benefits, and *their* well-being.[11]

As a Missouri editor put it, he would use "only those news releases which have a local angle."

Editors seem unconcerned with the difficulties a campaign would have in targeting releases for each local area different papers serve. To them, it seems a minor task to highlight a local name, emphasize a local issue, or stress a local concern: "Since they have our address, they should send us just those comments the candidate makes which would concern our area." They think that localized releases will serve their readers better, and so it is probable that such releases are more readily used. The problem for the campaigner, of course, is that only one or two papers would be likely to use such a release, and there is a chance that a release with a more general appeal would be used by ten to twenty papers. Perhaps, said one editor, that explains why "*No* candidate has yet found a way to make use of the local media; nor have they ever taken any suggestions on localizing their news."

There are also a number of suggestions for improving the content of the releases, most of them general: "Being relevant," from a Minnesota editor; "More background—less B.S.," from an Iowa editor; and "Make them more informational," from another Iowa editor. But the dissatisfaction is not as great on this score as I had expected. But some editors are caustic. For example, how can campaign press releases be most improved? "They are by nature promoting a particular viewpoint. Can a leopard change its spots?" asked a Pennsylvania editor. Certainly, the editors complain about the "ego-building bologna which most p-r people put in releases and all newspaper editors should take out," but editors expect self-serving statements from all news sources, and press releases are no different. One New Jersey editor had no complaint on content: "For the most part I find political news releases done rather well in this respect. They usually hit on issues at hand." A small-town Nebraska editor does not expect campaign releases to improve in content at all; it would defeat the candidate's purpose:

It would be unrealistic to expect a candidate to be controversial in a news release. He is seeking favorable notoriety, not argument. They will be truthful as long as the truth doesn't hurt. I suppose that is true of you and I [sic] also. We don't want our illusions disturbed.[12]

Weekly editors made a point of suggesting that release writers take their special needs into account. The problem is that the deadlines for weeklies are different from those for dailies, so releases sent to both dailies and weeklies are no longer news when the weekly has the opportunity to use them. Weeklies do not appreciate that fact: "We don't like to be a *history* 'sheet.' "

A number of editors also made suggestions concerning the connection between advertising and releases. One Wisconsin editor reported that he has "often heard other area editors moan as to why more candidates do not *buy* ad space . . . perhaps one indicater as to why so little early political press releases reach print." To many editors, campaign press releases are advertising in disguise and should therefore be replaced with paid ads. Virtually all of the suggestions for improving campaign press releases by replacing them with advertisements came from weekly editors—they may, in their smaller operations, be more concerned with and aware of the problems associated with selling advertising in their papers and the need for the revenue those advertisements produce.

Editing releases can be a headache. Quite a few editors noted that release writers should learn something about journalistic style. Editors prefer the "inverted pyramid" style, where the most important information is placed on the opening paragraphs, with less important facts lower in the story. Editors can then fit the release to available space by eliminating paragraphs from the end of the story as necessary. "Since space is often at premium, articles written with main gist in first paragraphs have more chance of being printed than if at end—should be able to cut at each paragraph," according to a New Jersey weekly editor. The advice is good: if a candidate wants to maximize his chances of having his releases used, he should follow good journalistic format. Reducing the editor's work will increase the probability that the release will be used.

Other suggestions from editors cannot be easily categorized. Some point out that the writing can be much improved. An Iowa editor suggested that release writers "develop better leads—not 'charged,' 'accused.' " An editor from Minnesota suggested that releases should have "fewer 'pat-on-the-back' quotes." A North Dakota editor said that release writers "need to keep in mind the basic who, what, when, where, and why." In additional comments, he suggested that "It would seem to be a whole lot simpler and better if we were simply told, 'He came, he saw, he conquered, ate a plate of beans and left.' " Releases written well are less likely to be used for, as a California daily editor commented, "mopping up spilled coffee."

A Wisconsin weekly editor made an additional suggestion, one that I have not seen in works on preparing news releases or in responses by other editors to these questionnaires. He proposed simply that "envelopes could be annotated for easier handling; otherwise, when received in a group, [they] are hardly considered." The idea is straightforward and one that is already in use to some extent by some candidates. John Anderson's news releases in 1980, for instance, were sent out in envelopes identifying the contents as campaign releases. But the editor, I think, means somewhat more detailed annotation. If the editor can tell from the envelope that the news release enclosed deals with his circulation area, he may be much more likely to open that envelope immediately. Smaller campaign operations that do not send out their releases in specially marked envelopes could adapt their procedures easily with good prospects for better use of their releases.

An advantage for candidates of reaching voters through campaign press releases is to make the resulting communication seem an impartial, reporter-originated news story, as has been noted. Editors were asked in the national survey whether they knew when a reporter based his news story on a campaign release; almost 90 percent "usually" or "always" knew. When they were asked, however, whether they thought readers knew whether a story was based on a release, less than 40 percent replied that they thought readers "usually" or "always" could, but exactly half of them thought readers "seldom" or "occasionally" could determine the real origin of the item. Of course, some editors may have overestimated the ability of their readers to smell out candidate propaganda, but a number of them may have underestimated the sensitivity of their readers to the sources behind news stories. The responses from editors who reported that their news stories always indicate when the item is based on a release may have inflated the assessment of the extent of readers' knowledge about candidate-inspired news items. But it is not accurate to say, based on these editors' responses, that candidates are frustrated in their attempts to reach voters through impartial-looking news stories by calling the reader's attention to the actual source of the news.

In summary, releases are used, even though editors respond unfavorably to them. Some releases, of course, evoke worse responses than others. The unfavorable responses are the product of clashing sets of standards. The purposes campaigners have in mind, as noted in chapter 1, are inconsistent with the needs of editors. Campaign press releases are propaganda, not news, and editors as well as candidates recognize that fact. Some releases, however, are less likely to be caught in that clash of standards; these are releases that contain some element of what editors call hard news and a minimum of propaganda. A short announcement of an appointment of a local notable to a campaign position, for instance, might meet editorial standards.

It seems that editors of weekly papers are less antagonistic toward campaign releases than are editors of dailies. Whether the reason is a relative paucity of news-gathering resources or lower standards for what constitutes news is difficult to say; it may be both. But to exploit this relatively favorable attitude, campaigners are caught in the general interest-local relevance dilemma alluded to earlier. One of the major advantages of campaign releases, their low cost, would soon be lost if a different release had to be prepared for virtually every newspaper in the constituency. One way out would be to prepare releases with regional relevance, a release that mentioned by name individuals in several communities. Weeklies should not be ignored in the preparation and distribution of releases, because readers of dailies can be reached through press conferences, regular news coverage, and media events, but weeklies rarely have the resources to expose the candidate to their readers if he does not stimulate the coverage himself.

Given the clashing standards, and given the fact that some releases are used, the main advice for campaigners that comes out of these surveys is not to make things worse. Pay attention to style, format, deadlines, and the organization of the release. It is difficult enough to persuade an editor to use a release. By adhering to professional journalistic standards as much as possible, the candidate can maximize the chances of his releases being used. After all, if a release requires little extra work on the part of the editor, he is more likely to commit space in the next issue to it. That prospect helps both editor and candidate.

6

THE RELEASES IN PRINT

The tension between journalistic standards for news and the desire of campaigners to stimulate favorable publicity need not work in favor of news people, even though the decision to use releases is theirs alone. By manipulating the campaign situation to their advantage and by capitalizing on the procedures reporters use to cover news, campaigners can get quite a few of their releases published. Campaigners and journalists influence each other, as F. Christopher Arterton pointed out in his description of the media coverage of the Carter nomination campaign.[1] Although the reporters' final choice about using releases seems to give them veto power over that means of reaching voters, their need for news—whether to satisfy readers, to gain a competitive advantage over other media, or to please superiors with their efficiency—leads them to accept and to use candidate news releases. In addition, since the campaign organizations themselves are almost the only sources of information about the campaign, the way in which they present campaign news defines the situation for reporters. As a result, if campaigners offer news in accordance with journalistic standards, it will be printed.

To be sure, not all attempts to stimulate news coverage are going to be successful. Some media events will draw no television cameras; some press releases will not be used. The difficulty for campaigners is predicting which releases will be accepted and which will be rejected. A daily check of the press covering the campaign can serve as a guide, but few campaigners have the time to do a thorough job on the matter.[2] A cursory check may not reveal sufficient information. Since releases can be used in a number of ways, campaigners would want to know how the releases they distributed are treated by the press.

Answers to the questions of which releases were used by the press and how the press used them are reported here based on an examination of the news stories stimulated by the Byrne, Sandman, Bailey, and Fithian releases. In addition, news stories generated by other releases in selected publications were also reviewed.[3]

The releases successfully accomplished their major objective: to stimulate substantial press coverage in the newspapers covering the campaigns. Such publicity, achieved at a relatively low cost, made releases an effective and efficient communication tool for the campaigns, even for campaigns that emphasized television too.

Explaining why some releases were used while others were not turned out to be relatively difficult—no one characteristic of the releases examined accounts for more than a minor portion of the variation. Use of releases, however, can be *partially* explained by their subject matter, length, newsworthiness, and the campaign week (for the Byrne and Sandman releases) in which they were issued. These factors were used to describe the releases in chapter 3. There I assumed that reporters would make their decisions to use releases quickly on the basis of obvious characteristics such as the above. That assumption is partially validated by the evidence.

Since candidates use releases as part of their overall communication with voters, they assign to releases goals that suit their capabilities. Some purposes that releases are commonly given—to generate publicity, to increase a candidate's name recognition, to help overcome an opponent's lead in the public opinion polls—can be performed by other communication techniques as well, although usually much more expensively. A related goal for releases is to stimulate coverage when the campaign wants it, that is, to produce a flow of news when the campaign requires publicity. The way in which the press used the Byrne, Sandman, Fithian, and Bailey releases made it possible for the candidates' goals to be met. The goals in question were general. It is unlikely that a release would have been sufficient if the goal were to publicize one candidate's position on a specific issue—the resulting coverage might be sparse. But these broad goals were realistic, and the press coverage the releases stimulated fit the candidates' needs.

The success Byrne and Sandman enjoyed with their news releases can be gauged from two simple indicators. Two hundred fifty-three of their 363 releases (69.7 percent) were used at least once by one of the papers serving New Jersey. These 253 releases were used 968 times, an average of 3.83 times per release. In other words, each release resulted in approximately four news stories, if the release was used at all. This amount of publicity vindicates those who believe in press releases.

Indiana's Floyd Fithian did even better. Seven of his nine releases were used at least once by papers covering his congressional district, a success rate of 77.8 percent. However, his releases generated fewer stories each. Those seven releases were used a total of 24 times, or 3.43 uses per release. Wendell Bailey of Missouri did not fare as well as Fithian in the percentage of releases picked up by papers in his congressional district. But the figure was still higher than it was for Byrne and Sandman; forty-five of his sixty releases were used at least once. Bailey was successful, however, in getting more than one paper to use his releases. His releases stimulated 195 uses, an average of 4.33 per release used. These rates of use compare favorably to what Kaid found in her study of the campaign releases issued by an Illinois legislative candidate.[4]

Neither Byrne nor Sandman gained much of an advantage over the other in the use of their releases, since similar numbers of releases were used. Of Byrne's 179 releases, 125 were used at least once (69.8 percent), as were 128 of Sandman's 184 releases (69.6 percent). Each candidate's releases resulted in approximately the same number of stories per release being used as well. Sandman's 128 releases produced 499 news stories, for an average of 3.90 per release, and Byrne's 125 releases resulted in 469 news stories, for an average of 3.75 uses per release. The differences between the candidates are not statistically significant.

Another measure of success in generating publicity is the frequency with which stories based on the releases used the candidates' names in the headlines. Since newspaper readers choose which stories to read on the basis of the headlines (as well as placement of the stories), and since headlines are widely read, even by those who may not read the stories themselves, such exposure is valuable. Over three-fourths (78.0 percent) of the 852 items based on the releases mentioned one or both of the candidates' names in the headlines.[5] Sandman had a definite edge, having his name included in 353 headlines alone and in 36 headlines together with Byrne's name. Byrne, on the other hand, had only 277 headline mentions alone. But only 4 of the 24 items using Fithian releases did not use the candidate's name in the headline, for a use rate of 83.3 percent. Bailey's releases got the candidate's name in the headlines frequently as well; 133 times out of the 179 news stories based on the releases were run with Bailey's name being prominent.

The releases stimulated substantial coverage then. It does not follow, however, that there were no important differences in content between the releases that appeared in some form in the press and those that did not. In fact, the differences were minor. The rejected releases were as likely to be concerned with images and with issues, for example, as the releases that were used. If the messages the candidates wanted to send the electorate did not reach them, it was not because crucial releases were not used. Whether the messages got through to the voters depended more on the way the press treated the releases than on their choice of which releases to use.

Since content does not account for the fact that some releases were used while others were not, the impact of other factors must be considered. There are some differences between used and rejected releases in release category, length, campaign week, and newsworthiness, as well as differences between the use of releases from the candidates within some of these classifications.

Taking the Byrne and Sandman releases together, there are few differences in the percentage of releases from each of the four release categories (candidate statements, campaign appointments, endorsements, and miscellaneous releases) the press used. The press was no more likely to use candidate statements than announcements of appointments to the campaign. The rates of use ranged from 74.3 percent of campaign appointments to 63.2 percent of miscellaneous releases. The differences are not statistically significant.

Looking at the releases from the candidates separately, however, reveals more substantial differences. The differences in use of releases for Sandman ranged from 93.3 percent for endorsement releases to 59.5 percent for miscellaneous releases. For Byrne, the range was from 54.2 percent (endorsement) to 83.0 percent (candidate statements). There is, in other words, an interaction effect. Although we found little difference in use of releases when we compared the candidates and when we compared categories, there are obvious differences when candidates and categories are compared simultaneously. Which candidate issued a release in which category influenced the press's decision to use it.

Comparison with the use of Bailey's releases by category is instructive. However, a direct comparison with Byrne and Sandman is inappropriate, because a completely different set of newspapers is involved. Much of the variation noted may be due to varying press characteristics rather than to features of the releases. The use of Bailey's releases ranged from 60.0 percent of his ten candidate statements to 91.3 percent of his endorsement releases (disregarding the 100.0 percent in the campaign-appointment category, since it was based on use of one release only). Use of his miscellaneous releases is similar to the use of the New Jersey candidates' releases in this category: 65.4 percent. The way the Missouri press used his releases resembled the use of the Sandman releases more than the Byrne releases by the New Jersey press.

Release length was associated with use. Since the editors responding to the questionnaires, as reported in the previous chapter, suggested that length was a relevant criterion in their decisions to use releases, and since they cited space availability as a major consideration as well, one would expect to find differences in the way the press used long and short campaign press releases.[6] Specifically, the editors suggested that shorter releases have a better chance of being used. Unfortunately, if anything, the evidence shows that longer releases were used more frequently than shorter ones. Two sets of data support this conclusion.

The first set involves the use the press made of the longest and shortest releases that Byrne and Sandman issued, a total of 175 releases (48 percent of the total). More than twice as many short releases were rejected as long releases. Almost half again as many long releases were used as short releases. A similar conclusion can be drawn from the use of Byrne's long and short releases alone, but for Sandman, the relationship is not nearly so strong, although it is still contrary to the original expectation—for Sandman, too, longer releases were more likely to be used. See table 6.1.

The second set of evidence comes from calculating the correlations between length and release use, but the results are less clear-cut. The overall relationship is still there ($r = .142$ between length and a dichotomous variable—whether the release was used or not—and $r = .172$ between length and the number of times the release was used) when the New Jersey candidates' releases are considered together. The correlation coefficient between length and the dichotomous use variable was .134 for the use of Bailey's releases, a value

Table 6.1:   Press Use of Long and Short Releases (New Jersey Candidates)

	CANDIDATES					
LENGTH	Byrne		Sandman		Both	
	Releases Used	Releases Not Used	Releases Used	Releases Not Used	Releases Used	Releases Not Used
Short	22	20	28	15	50	35
Long	38	7	35	10	73	17
Total	60	27	63	25	123	52

Source: Computed from releases and clippings supplied by the candidates or their campaign staffs.

Note: For Byrne: $X^2 = 8.99$, $p < .025$, 1 df, Yule's $Q = .633$. For Sandman: $X^2_y = 1.17$, $p < .30$, 1 df, Yule's $Q = .304$. For both: $X^2_y = 9.36$, $p < .005$, 1 df, Yule's $Q = .501$.

comparable to Byrne's and Sandman's. But the association is smaller between length and the number of times a release is used, only .096. (Fithian's values, based as they are on only nine releases, are much less reliable; the dichotomous variable and length correlated more strongly—$r = .263$. The reason is simply that the most widely used Fithian release was the one in which he announced his intention to seek reelection; that release was at the same time the shortest.) It is not likely that length would explain much of the variation in the press-use variable, and it does not. The relationship is contrary to the direction the editors pointed out.

The time when a release is issued during a campaign can be expected to be related to its chance of being used. Simply because campaign interest is higher in the later stages, one would expect that releases coming out then would be more likely to stimulate news coverage. Only the Byrne and Sandman data can be applied here, since Bailey neglected to date his releases, and because Fithian issued so few. There is a small but negative correlation between campaign week and the dichotomous use of releases variable ($r = -.097$) when Sandman's and Byrne's releases are combined. There is virtually no difference between the results for Byrne and Sandman on this score. The results on the other measure, the number of times a release is used, are different. The overall r value is -.190, but Byrne's is quite a bit larger than Sandman's, -.377 versus -.111. The rate at which the press used releases did not increase as the campaign went on—in fact, it declined slightly.

Newsworthiness alone was virtually unrelated to a release's chance of being used. The correlation between a release's newsworthiness score and the number of times the New Jersey press used it was a meager .084. The fact that the association is even as strong as this is because of Byrne's releases. The correlation for his releases was $r = .183$, but the correlation for Sandman's releases was virtually zero—$r = .010$. For Bailey's releases, the result was similar: $r = .097$. Again, Fithian was somewhat of an exception. The correlation coefficient between release use and newsworthiness for his releases was a strong .590, but again because of the small number of releases, the figure is not very meaningful.

However, since the newsworthiness index is computed by adding the releases's scores on five components, the total may hide some variation among the releases on individual components, variation that may affect its chance of being used. The result of a multiple correlation between release use and each of the components is better. The multiple correlation coefficient, for example, for Byrne's releases rose to a respectable .270, and Sandman's R reached even higher: .344. Bailey's coefficient also rose, to a moderate .214, but Fithian's stayed approximately the same: $R = .598$. Again, Fithian's result must be discounted, because using five variables to explain the use of nine releases will yield high correlations as a matter of course. To use the index in this way, rather than as a cumulative figure, gives us a little more confidence both in its utility and in the professional standards of journalists.

The component that accounted for most of the variance was the unexpectedness factor. The beta for this component in a multiple regression between the number of times the releases were used for both New Jersey candidates and the five components was 3.18, indicating that a release containing unexpected news was likely to be used three instances more than a release without such news. The strength of this factor, in comparison with the others, suggests that it encompasses what editors and reporters consider news more clearly than do the other components. No other factor came close to having this kind of impact. The complete regression equation was:

$$\text{Release Use} = .43\,T - .43\,C + .05\,I + 3.18\,U + .44\,VIP + 2.06,$$

where T is timeliness, C is conflict, I is impact, U is unexpectedness, and VIP is the involvement of prominent people. None of the

Fithian or Bailey releases scored any points on the unexpectedness component.

Of interest, too, is the fact that an element of the conflict factor in the regression is of approximately the same magnitude as the impact of timeliness and of the involvement of important people. For both Bailey and Fithian, however, the sign of the coefficient in the multiple regression equations is positive. Bailey's coefficient is a sizable 2.40, and Fithian's coefficient is 4.00 (with, however, a standard error of 3.61). In New Jersey, then, releases that avoid conflict stand a better chance of being used, but in other states such as Missouri and Indiana, an element of conflict may just spark the editor's interest.

Length, campaign week, and newsworthiness individually account for very little of the variance in the use of the Byrne and Sandman releases. The campaign-week variable explains about 14 percent of the variance in the use of Byrne's releases, but that is the most any of these factors account for. Combining these three variables raised the explanatory power: R for both candidates considered together reaches .308. When the newsworthiness index is replaced by its five components in the multiple correlation, the coefficient for the two candidates combined becomes .392, but Byrne's multiple R is .517, which means these seven measures together explain 27 percent of the variance. The result for Sandman is .364, explaining 13 percent of the variance.

It would have been nice to have been able to explain much more of the variation in press use of these releases. Such an explanation would have aided campaigners in the preparation of their releases and provided a firmer foundation for their decisions about releases. The evidence, however, explains only part of it. Nevertheless, enough of the disparity in use is accounted for to justify the rejection of the notion that press use of releases is basically random. There is at least some pattern.

As the evidence reported in chapter 3 demonstrated, Byrne issued more releases than Sandman did in the early part of the campaign (indeed, Byrne had put out thirty-eight more releases than Sandman had by the fourteenth week of the campaign), and Sandman distributed more than Byrne did in the later part of the campaign. A putative advantage for Byrne was the possibility that he would stimulate greater news coverage than Sandman during the first half of the campaign, when Byrne needed to build name recognition with New Jersey voters. Sandman's late flood of releases may have been inspired by the public opinion polls, which showed him losing at that point.[7] Neither Byrne nor Sandman's goals, however, could have been attained if the press did not use the releases in a pattern similar to the rate at which they were issued.

Therefore, one would expect that there would be a corresponding advantage for Byrne in the cumulative number of news stories based on his releases published during the campaign. Figure 6.1 demonstrates that this conclusion is correct. At one point during the campaign (at the end of the eleventh week), there had been 152 more stories based on Byrne releases than items based on Sandman releases in the New Jersey press, 243 for Byrne but only 91 for Sandman. It was not until after the sixteenth week that Byrne's

FIGURE 6.1: CUMULATIVE NUMBER OF NEWS ITEMS BASED ON
BYRNE RELEASES MINUS CUMULATIVE NUMBER
OF NEWS ITEMS BASED ON SANDMAN RELEASES
BY CAMPAIGN WEEK

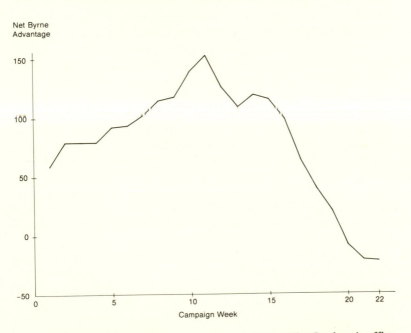

Source: Computed from clippings supplied by Representative Sandman's office.

advantage in the number of news stories used dropped below 100. Sandman's attempt to stimulate coverage by issuing many press releases began in earnest at that point, and he obtained substantial publicity from news releases, compared to Byrne, later in the campaign. Byrne's earlier concentration of releases, then, benefited him to the extent that he was able to get a larger number of stories based on his releases published during the summer than was Sandman. But later in the campaign, Sandman's flood of releases gained him the exposure in the press he wanted. There seems, then, to be a close association between the rate at which releases are issued and the rate at which they are used. The fact makes it possible for candidate strategies such as Byrne's and Sandman's to succeed.[8]

If releases are to be worth using, they usually must be published relatively promptly, for old news has little attraction. The number of days between the date a release is made available and the date the news story based on it appears should be relatively small if the release is to serve specific candidate purposes.[9] Since both dailies and weeklies received releases, one would expect that campaign press releases, when used, would be used on the average approximately three or four days after they are made available.

Actual use comes close to this expectation. An average of 3.94 days elapsed before the appearance of news items based on the releases. The difference between Byrne and Sandman is surprisingly large. It took an average of 4.33 days for a Sandman release to see the light of day, but only 3.53 days for a Byrne release. This suggests that Byrne may have had somewhat better success in using releases to meet his goals—they were used while the news was still fresher than was true for Sandman's releases. But the figures for both candidates were quite a bit lower than for press use of Fithian's releases. It took, on average, almost a week for a news story based on his releases to appear: 6.63 days. In part, however, this high figure was due to one publication, the *Daneland Journal,* which used one release 33 days after it was issued; without that instance, the figure is 5.48 days.

There is, at best, slight evidence that newsworthy releases serve candidates better in this regard. It is likely that the press would use newsworthy releases more promptly than releases that had less to recommend them. The data support this assumption, although the proportion of the variance explained is negligible. The association between the newsworthiness index score and the number of days between release date and press use should be negative, and that is indeed the result for the New Jersey candidates. The correlation for Sandman's releases is -.148, and for Byrne's it is -.174. Although the correlations are not high, they are gratifying in the right direction. Again, Fithian is an exception, but the correlation between the index and the number of days elapsed before release use is almost zero: $r = .030$.

Since some releases were not used, an attempt to account for the pattern of use is in order. The framework used in chapter 3 suggested that reporters decide relatively quickly whether to use a release on the basis of factors they can readily discern. The analysis has indicated that these factors account only partially for the pattern of use. Several explanatory points can be raised.

First, newsworthiness, as measured by the index, turned out to be a poor predictor of use. Before the measure is discarded, however, we should consider whether newsworthiness is likely to be that good a predictor. Space availability, for instance, may account for much more release use; unfortunately, measuring the impact of that factor is beyond the scope of this study. In any case, a low correlation between newsworthiness and release use is a significant conclusion. It suggests that decisions to use releases are not based primarily on the considerations journalists use to defend their customary choices.

Newsworthiness of releases, as noted in chapter 3, is low overall. Campaigners find different formats more convenient and effective to report significant developments. The upshot is that the differences between releases on newsworthiness are relatively minor; even a release with a comparatively high score on the index is low in news value. Furthermore, releases must compete with other campaign news and, late in the campaign, with many other campaign releases with basically similar newsworthiness scores. Under such conditions, slight differences in newsworthiness do not serve to distinguish releases, and other factors may come into play—first come, first served, for instance.

In addition, the index did not include one factor that editors cited regularly as a major consideration in their decisions to use releases: local interest. A release intended for statewide (or even for regional) distribution could not be given a score based on its "local" interest, since that value would differ from locality to locality. The index, therefore, understates the impact of news values on release use.

Since releases do stimulate substantial publicity for the candidate, their potential for reaching the electorate is noteworthy, but that potential is not necessarily equivalent to the potential for communicating messages to voters. A large portion of the electorate may not read newspaper stories based on candidate news releases at all, or the messages in releases may not survive the transition from release to newspaper copy. The messages in one-third of the releases did not reach any audience at all (except the reporter or editor who scrapped the release). Some of the other releases were cut drastically before the press printed them. Charges of press bias, press manipulation of news, and press distortion of public pronouncements by public figures are not new, nor are they totally unfounded. Changes in press releases a reporter or editor makes may very well be seen as distortion by the candidate or as evidence of newspaper bias against him and in favor of his opponent. One reason for such a response is that each candidate is perfectly aware of the alterations the press makes in his releases before using them, but he is aware only of the fact that his opponent's releases are being used.

Because space is at a premium, no newspaper can print all of the releases it receives. The press is often faced with the choice of ignoring a release or cutting it to fit the available space. The editorial writer for the *Glen Ridge* (New Jersey) *Paper* discussed this point:

Every morning a batch of releases by political candidates comes in the mail. There seems to be no consideration of how much a weekly newspaper can use and generally we have to restrict publication to one statement per week from each candidate.

Of greatest interest usually are the releases from the candidates for Governor. They seize on almost any issue to get statements in the paper as many days as possible. Some of the issues are pretty thin because they are trying so hard to get the attention of the public, but some of the statements do contain interesting new ideas.[10]

If the papers cannot use all of the releases, one might expect them to use parts of some, so that they could use more releases (and other news) than if they printed them in toto. One would expect that the press would not hesitate to edit the releases to use as many of the "statements [with] interesting new ideas" as possible.[11] That means cutting the releases.

Cutting the releases may mean diluting the message the candidate is concerned with. (Sometimes, however, a good editor can clarify the message of a release by removing excess verbiage.) Consider, for example, a typical campaign press release announcing the appointment of Leslie Glick to a position in the Byrne campaign:

Glick Named Chairman of Byrne Committee

Leslie P. Glick, a Cranford attorney, Thursday was named Chairman of the Ex-Law Enforcement Officials Committee for Byrne, by Brendan T. Byrne, Democratic candidate for Governor.

In making the appointment, Byrne stated, "I have known Les Glick for many years and am well acquainted with his outstanding legal background and record as a trial attorney and prosecutor. I am pleased he has accepted the chairmanship of this very important committee."

"It is a distinct privilege for me to head this vital phase of Brendan's campaign," Glick said. "It is my sincere belief that he will restore honesty and integrity to state government.

"New Jersey needs Brendan Byrne. He will make a great leader and governor," Glick said.

Glick, a member of the Cranford law firm of Rubenstein and Glick, has served as an Assistant Union County Prosecutor. He has been Cranford Municipal Chairman since 1971 and is active in the Cranford Rotary Club. He was President of the Cranford Lodge, B'nai B'rith in 1972.

The Committee will sponsor a fund-raising luncheon at noon on Wednesday, October 17 at the Coachman Inn in Cranford. Former U.S. Attorney David M. Satz, Jr. and the former State Attorney General Arthur J. Sills are among those serving on the state-wide committee.[12]

This release includes at least two blatant attempts to appeal to voters with a message. The first is aimed at those who might be able to identify with the appointee, because they share his outlook, because they share his background (for example, ethnic, professional, and geographic), or because they belong to similar groups (such as the Lions Club or Kiwanis). The praise of the appointee becomes praise as well for those who, like him, devote time and energy to the campaign for Byrne. The inference is that good Rotarians, and so forth, are Byrne supporters. The second message is aimed at those who need reassurance about the candidate. The virtues Glick sees in Byrne may or may not exist, but the fact that someone other than Byrne refers to them explicitly makes it easier for the reader to swallow the hyperbole, or so the argument would go. Byrne must be worthy of support if Glick sees so many good qualities in him.

Newspaper editors and reporters are likely to be unimpressed with a release of this type. In fact, this release can be easily boiled down to one or two paragraphs, if the concern is for its news value. The fact that Glick has been appointed to a position in the Byrne campaign and that his position entails these various duties is usually all that the press is interested in (unless the appointment is startling, such as the appointment of a member of the other party or a leader of an interest group that was expected to support the opponent). In other words, the essential message that the press is concerned with communicating to its readers is markedly different from the message the candidate and his campaign organization would like to put across. Sometimes, however, the press will help. A newspaper may highlight the fact that the appointee is a local person, in which case the message conveyed will more than likely evoke a sympathetic response, since the readers will receive a different message—Glick, a local man, is appointed to a position in the Byrne campaign. In either case, whether the press boils the release down to its basic news value or whether it emphasizes the involvement of a local notable, the message conveyed by the press is likely to be different from the original message in the release. Is this distortion? It is hard to say.

Before we come to a specific examination of the changes the press made in their use of campaign releases, it is necessary to classify the kinds of changes they made. Basically, papers give releases six categories of treatments. The first one is to print the releases exactly (or nearly so) as they were provided by the candidates. Quite a few releases examined for this study were used verbatim; exact figures are cited later. Second, the releases could be used exactly as they were issued (or with minor changes), but the concluding paragraphs could be omitted. Such changes often occur for space reasons. Third, a release could be used virtually as issued, but with paragraphs missing from the middle of the release. In this case, content could be a consideration in the mind of the editor. In all three of these treatments, most if not all of the language in the news release will have survived in the news story.

The other three categories of handling campaign releases involve changing the wording of the releases. The fourth method is substantially to rewrite the releases. In this case, the reporter either paraphrases the original, or he begins from scratch, taking the facts and the information and putting it into his own words, often leaving out portions of the release. The fifth method is summary; releases are often summarized, usually to shorten the message and to report the basic news content (an endorsement, an appointment, and so forth) without the added baggage of self-serving statements that editors dislike and distrust. The "other" ways of treating releases comprise the sixth category. Most common among the treatments included here is the news story based on a public event, such as an appearance by the candidate at a rally or a meeting, about which a release is also made available. It is impossible to determine if a reporter is using his own notes when he quotes the candidate, if that quotation is also in the release, or if he is using the release. But the release may have been significant to the reporter when he wrote his account of the event. He may have used none of the information, none of the words, and none of the release's organization, and yet it may have influenced the way in which he perceived the event he was reporting, whether negatively or positively. He may have quoted the candidate in a particular instance, because the release also quoted him. It is therefore possible that the release had an impact on the final news story.

These six kinds of treatment that a candidate's news releases could receive from the press are not steps on a scale measuring the degree to which the final news item distorted or changed the content of the release. Such a scale would make the analysis here a great deal easier; however, none is practical. William Martin and Michael Singletary used a different method to examine press treatment of releases, in their case, releases issued by a Pennsylvania state agency. Their technique (they "counted the number of complete sentences appearing in the newspaper article that were identical to the news release, and divided the identical . . . sentences by the total number of sentences in the article"[13]) would yield misleading results in this study. Too many newspaper articles incorporate a candidate news release virtually verbatim into longer campaign stories. The Martin and Singletary technique would classify such use of releases as if the release were greatly changed, but the technique I use here accurately indicates that the candidate's message in the release found its way into print, despite whatever else the reporter may have put into the news story.

To be sure, one might expect that verbatim use of a release would not change the message, that dropping a paragraph is better for the candidate than having the release summarized, and that a rewrite would probably change the content less than one of the treatments in the sixth category would. But it is not true that a message is more likely to come through undistorted if paragraphs are dropped at the end of a release rather than in the middle—that would depend on the content of those paragraphs. Similarly, one rewrite might distort a release's meaning, and another might reflect it quite well. These treatments are "nominal," not "ordinal" variables.

The treatment candidates would prefer, of course, is to have releases used verbatim, or nearly so. Of the 968 different uses made of the Byrne and Sandman releases, 148, or 15.3 percent, were verbatim copies of the releases in question. By contrast, 38.5 percent of the uses of Bailey's releases were verbatim, and 50.0 percent of the uses of Fithian's releases were verbatim. The differences between Byrne and Sandman in verbatim use of their releases is noteworthy: 16.6 percent (83) of the 499 uses of Sandman's releases were verbatim printings, but only 13.9 percent (65) of the 469 uses of Byrne's releases fell into this category. One major observation is that releases announcing appointments to positions in local campaign organizations were most likely to be accorded verbatim treatment: 36.4 percent of the uses of the Sandman and Byrne releases in this category were verbatim. That about 1 release use out of 7 was a verbatim use indicates a relatively substantial number of releases reach newspaper readers with their messages intact. That this is a substantial number is a judgment that depends on one's expectations, but one cannot realistically expect too many releases to undergo so little editing, given the replies editors gave to the questions on the surveys analyzed in the previous chapter.

Taking the first three treatments together (verbatim use, verbatim with end paragraphs dropped, and verbatim with middle paragraphs dropped) makes more precise statements possible. Sandman's releases were much more likely to receive one of these three types of treatment than were Byrne's releases. Almost 39 percent of the uses of Sandman's releases (193) fell into these categories, compared with only 23 percent (109) of the uses of Byrne's releases. The difference is marked.

There is also a significant difference in the distribution of these three uses among the four categories of releases described in chapter 3. In three of the four categories, Sandman's releases were more

likely to be used verbatim, but endorsement releases issued by
Byrne were more likely to be used verbatim or nearly so than those
issued by Sandman. Byrne, however, had a greater number of
endorsement releases in the first place. Reexamining those figures
in the light of total use, the difference is not so great: 27.7 percent
of the uses of Byrne's endorsement releases fell into these treatment
categories, compared with 19.6 percent for the uses of Sandman's
endorsements. See table 6.2. Local campaign appointment releases
(part of the overall campaign appointment category) deserve separate comment. More than half of all uses of these releases were given
one of the first three treatments; in fact, for Sandman, the percentage is 67.2 percent. It seems that if local campaign appointment releases were going to be used by the New Jersey press, they
were most likely to be used as they were written by the candidates,
or with relatively minor changes.

Many of the uses were summaries; almost 20.0 percent of all uses
in the Byrne and Sandman campaigns were summaries. But for the
Fithian and Bailey releases, summaries were uncommon, with only
4.0 percent of Bailey's uses falling into this category and one use

Table 6.2:   Treatments 1 through 3 by Candidate and Category
             (New Jersey Candidates)

CATEGORY	BYRNE	SANDMAN	TOTAL
Candidate statements	27	67	94
Campaign appointments	34	82	116
Endorsements	31	11	42
Miscellaneous	17	33	50
Total	109	193	302

Source: Compiled from clippings supplied by Representative Sandman's office.
Note: The treatments are (1) verbatim use, (2) verbatim use with end paragraphs
dropped, and (3) verbatim use with middle paragraphs dropped.

of Fithian's. Differences between Sandman and Byrne on this score are inconsequential: 19.6 percent of all uses for Sandman and 18.3 percent for Byrne. The reason so many uses are in this category is that it is very simple to use a release by summarizing it. The editor does not need a separate news item, since he can tack a half-sentence summary on to a longer story. A release summary can become an item in itself, frequently no more than two paragraphs long, a filler at best, or it can be incorporated into a longer story, sometimes on an unrelated topic, sometimes in what is known as a roundup, a summary of campaign news, for example. One would expect that summaries are most likely to be used by daily newspapers that use wire services or that have reporters of their own. Weeklies, with small reportorial staffs, are probably more likely to have to use releases, if at all, as they come from the candidates, or with minor revisions. The releases that are most susceptible to summarizing are endorsement and campaign-appointment announcements, because the central fact of those releases can be easily and succinctly presented.

The number of "other" treatments, the sixth category, was also large: 232 of 968 uses of the New Jersey releases fell into this classification, or 24.0 percent of the total. All 14 uses of the Anderson releases by the big dailies of the nation were "other" treatments, and over 21.0 percent of the uses of the Bailey releases were of this sort. Candidate statements seem to warrant one of these treatments disproportionally, probably because they were more likely to issue releases in conjunction with public appearances. Of the 232 uses involved in the New Jersey data, 119 were candidate statements, 55 for Byrne and 64 for Sandman. Overall, a higher percentage of the uses of Byrne's releases received one of these treatments—26.7 percent, or 125 of 469 uses—than did Sandman's—21.4 percent, or 107 of 499 uses.

The conclusion is warranted that the New Jersey press used the campaign news releases issued by Sandman and Byrne in different ways. Sandman's releases were more likely to be used verbatim or nearly so, and Byrne's releases were more likely to receive one of the treatments in the sixth category. Byrne's releases were also much more likely to be rewritten (25.8 percent) than were Sandman's (20.2 percent).

Contrary to expectations, earlier results suggested that long releases were slightly more likely to be used than were short releases.

Tentatively, I advanced the hypothesis that shorter releases would be more likely than longer ones to be used verbatim, or nearly so. That hypothesis is supported by the data. With the treatment variable collapsed into two categories, with the first three kinds of treatment in one category and the other three kinds in another, it becomes clear that although some long releases were used verbatim and some short releases were summarized, short releases were more likely to be used verbatim or verbatim with paragraphs removed than were long releases. The relationship is clearer for Sandman than for Byrne. In Sandman's case, a majority of the uses of his shorter releases fell into the verbatim category, but for Byrne, only 30.0 percent of his short release uses were verbatim, or nearly so. For both candidates, verbatim uses were more likely to be accorded short than long releases, and the other treatments were more likely to be given to long releases, by a wide margin. Table 6.3 presents the data for Byrne and Sandman combined. The result for the Missouri candidate, Bailey, was similar—only 26.7 percent of his long releases received one of the variations of verbatim treatment, but almost 61.0 percent of his short releases did.

Does the week in the campaign when a release is used have any impact on the way that a release is treated? Do releases used early in the campaign stand a better chance of being used verbatim? The answers are no to both questions. Although there is some variation from week to week in the percentage of release uses falling into one

Table 6.3: Treatment of Releases by Length (New Jersey Candidates Combined)

TREATMENT[a]	LENGTH			TOTAL
	Short	Medium	Long	
1-3	72	162	68	302
4-6	105	307	254	666
Total	177	469	322	968

Source: Computed from clippings supplied by Representative Sandman's office.
Note: $X^2 = 25.10$, $p < .001$, 2 df, $C = .159$.

a. The treatments are (1) verbatim use, (2) verbatim use with end paragraphs dropped, (3) verbatim use with middle paragraphs dropped, (4) rewrites, (5) summaries, and (6) other treatments.

category in the New Jersey campaign, there is no discernible pattern. That variation is no doubt due to the impact of other factors, probably in most cases the subject matter and the newsworthiness of the releases being considered for use that week, but newspapers did not respond differently to these releases depending on the phase of the campaign during which they were used.

Since there was a substantial range in the number of days from the date a release was made available to the press and the time it was actually used in the newspaper, the difference in elapsed time may be related to the way in which newspapers actually treated the releases. In other words, are the releases that find their way into print relatively quickly used differently from those releases that are not used for a substantial number of days? Surprisingly, the answer is yes. The longer the delay between the date of release and the date of publication, the more likely it is that the release will be used verbatim or verbatim with some paragraphs deleted. The use of Fithian's releases is a case in point. Ten of the twelve "delayed" uses of his releases were verbatim treatments, and the "prompt" uses divided evenly between verbatim treatment and treatments with greater reporter involvement. Even stronger evidence comes from the Byrne and Sandman data. Combining the two candidates' releases, and comparing releases used within two days of issue with those used seven or more days after the release came out, a strong relationship emerges: Cramer's V is .460, significant at .001. This relationship results because weeklies cannot use releases as rapidly as can dailies because of their less frequent deadlines and their greater likelihood of using releases verbatim, a point to be established in the next chapter.

In any event, a long delay before a release is used makes it more likely that it will be used close to the form in which it was made available to the press. The conclusion holds for the releases of the two New Jersey candidates separately as well. Cramer's V is .414 for Byrne and .483 for Sandman, both significant at the .001 level. There is, therefore, some consolation to the candidate whose releases do not get used promptly; later use of his releases is more likely to convey his message faithfully. The advantages of prompt use and exact use of releases seem to counteract each other.

As might be expected, a release's newsworthiness influences the way in which editors and reporters use it. Specifically, one would expect that newsworthy developments, whether reported by a campaign news release or announced at a public appearance, would be likely to lead a reporter to write his own story, perhaps embodying the release in his story and perhaps using part of it. In other words, it is likely that reporters and editors would use a newsworthy release as an opportunity to write a news story of their own rather than printing the release as it was issued. Conversely, releases reporters judge less newsworthy are more likely to be used substantially as they were provided if they are going to be used at all. These expectations are well supported by the evidence.

To simplify the computation, the treatment variable was again collapsed into two categories, one including the verbatim variations and the other the summary, rewrite, and "other" treatments, and the newsworthiness scores were divided into three ranges, scores of two or below, scores from three to five, and scores of six and above. The relationship is just as expected. Combining the results for Sandman and Byrne, more than one-half of the uses of releases scoring low on the newsworthiness index fell into the verbatim category, but only about one-fourth of releases scoring medium on the index and one-fifth scoring high did. Only 42 of 229 uses in the high newsworthiness category were verbatim. The relationship for each of the candidates separately supports this finding, but for each of the three levels of newsworthiness, Sandman's releases were more likely to be used verbatim or nearly so than Byrne's, which is consistent with earlier conclusions. Of course, it is to be expected that comparing daily and weekly papers on this matter will help to explain the result.

Generally, the result is in the same direction for Dailey's releases, but his releases varied so little on newsworthiness that no reliable conclusions can be drawn. Only two times, for instance, were releases rating six on the newsworthiness scale used, but there were 144 uses of releases scoring two or below. About 55 percent of the uses of his least newsworthy releases were verbatim, and 57.1 percent of the uses of the medium newsworthy releases were verbatim. The two other uses split evenly between the two categories.

The candidates disguised some of their propaganda to slip it past editors concerned with objective reporting. These devices, discussed in chapter 4, included the use of identifying phrases, issuing releases to coincide with public appearances where the candidate makes publicly the statement distributed to the press in the release, identifying the candidate with groups, and putting propaganda into quotations. The release quoted on page 99 contains a fine example of propaganda disguised by quotation marks: it was

Glick's "sincere belief that he [Byrne] will restore honesty and integrity to state government."[14] These devices, of course, were virtually unnecessary where papers normally use releases verbatim, but one might expect that, even there, editors decide which releases to use on the basis of their approximation to their conceptions of good journalism.[15] In general, the conclusion that these propaganda devices were effective is warranted, but some devices worked better than others.

Identifying phrases and group identifications, for example, were not very successful. Except in the cases of releases used verbatim, few identifying phrases survived the editorial process. When releases containing such phrases were summarized, the summary would usually be too concise to include them; when these releases were rewritten, the reporter or editor would usually eliminate the identifying phrases or substitute others of his own. Group identifications were generally unsuccessful for a different reason. Few of the endorsement releases announcing the support the New Jersey candidates received from groups were used in the first place.

Tying releases in with public appearances, however, was much more successful in generating coverage and in generating the type of coverage the candidates wanted. A sizable number of release uses involved public appearances by the candidates: forty-eight for Byrne and sixty-two for Sandman. All of the candidate-statement releases issued by Ronald Reagan and John Anderson that were examined involved a public appearance by the candidate. In some of these cases, of course, the public appearance might have been covered by the press anyway, but the fact that a release was issued to go along with the appearance can influence the coverage the press gives. Take, for instance, the release Ronald Reagan issued on May 14, 1980, criticizing President Jimmy Carter's handling of the unemployment situation in Michigan, hard-hit because of the problems in the auto industry. The *Los Angeles Times* article reported Reagan's visit to the Flint and Troy, Michigan, area and dealt with the charges Reagan made in the release, but most of the article was concerned with the effectiveness of Reagan's responses to questions put to him by the auto workers.[16] Without the public appearance, the charges in the release would not have appeared in the news story. Similarly, when Reagan visited Houston in early May 1980, the *Los Angeles Times* story focused attention on his views of the Iranian hostage crisis then in progress. Only one paragraph at the end of the item referred to the release Reagan had distributed dealing with the energy crisis.[17] Again, without the public appearance, the release would not have been used.

Sometimes issuing a release at a public appearance can be mishandled. For example, on October 3, 1973, Byrne visited the Green Street traffic circle on Route 1 in Woodbridge, New Jersey. The story filed by Allen F. Yoder for the *Woodbridge News Tribune* included quotations from the release issued by the Byrne staff in two of the first three paragraphs, but later in the story, Yoder added that "the candidate didn't even bother to read aloud his prepared comments."[18] The influence of a release over a newspaper that did not send a reporter to cover the candidate's appearance is no doubt greater; it would not know that the statement was never actually made.

But quotations were the most successful of these propaganda devices. Close to half of the release uses of each of the two New Jersey candidates included quotations taken from the releases, 228 of 469 for Byrne and 226 of 499 for Sandman. For instance, a release from Stanley E. Laffin, a Maine State representative running for a seat in the Maine Senate in 1980, announcing his candidacy contained one quotation ("I feel that my service in the House of Representatives has given me a thorough knowledge of state government and the needs of the people and I can now better serve my constituency from the State Senate"). Although the editor of the *Westbrook* (Maine) *American Journal* edited the release extensively, the June 4, 1980, issue of the paper included a story based on the release that quoted Laffin exactly.[19]

Part of the success of this device can be attributed to the norms and standards journalists set for their professional performance. Quotations are simultaneously evidence for the development they are reporting and a means of avoiding charges of bias. The opinion manifested in the quotation cannot be attributed to the reporter, at least not under the standards of journalistic professionalism to which reporters subscribe. To the extent that the candidates put campaign propaganda into quotations, this device helped them communicate their messages to the voters.

Quite a few quotations, however, were eliminated when the press used the releases. Some were deleted in the process of rewriting or when the releases were summarized, but summaries and rewrites do not retain much of the original content and organization of the releases. When paragraphs are dropped from otherwise verbatim uses, however, changing the content of the releases may have been an important consideration for editors. For instance, to cite one example where dropping paragraphs deleted an important part of the message a candidate had for voters, consider the way in which the *Bayonne* (New Jersey) *Facts* used the Sandman release announcing the appointment of Kearny Mayor Anthony Cavalier to be Hudson County chairman in the Sandman campaign.[20] The release in question included two paragraphs quoting Cavalier on his reasons for working for Sandman. They are worth repeating, because they summarize concisely the major points Sandman wanted to emphasize in his campaign:

Cavalier said: "The voters in Hudson County are on the same side of the issues with Congressman Sandman. He's opposed to an income tax, and so are they. He wants home rule and is opposed to state-wide zoning being forced on them, and the voters feel the same way."

Cavalier said, "There is a distinct difference between Congressman Sandman and his opponent. Sandman was *elected* by the people in his successful public life as a State Senator and Congressman. His opponent was handpicked to jobs, and has no experience to solve the problems of this state."[21]

But the *Facts* item contained neither of these paragraphs. The impact of the report, therefore, did not extend to the image building that the release was partly devoted to.

As noted before, an editor may decide to delete one or more paragraphs from a release before using it for one of two reasons. The first reason is space availability. To the extent that the people who write news releases follow the journalistic precept that news stories should be written so that they can be cut from the bottom, that is, written so that each succeeding paragraph is less important than the preceding one and so that one or more paragraphs at the end can be dropped without losing the point of the story, then paragraphs dropped from the end of releases are probably cut mainly for space reasons.[22] However, when editors use a release in the form in which it was issued but delete paragraphs from the middle of the release, a consideration beside space availability was probably involved. Such deletions are evidence of choice among elements of the release, and such choices no doubt involve the editors' reactions to the content of the release. The way the *Bayonne Facts* treated the Sandman release is a good example.

Recall from chapter 4 that Byrne's releases stressed his honesty, his experience, and his responsiveness to the people, and Sandman emphasized his experience and his consistency on the issues. Bailey accented his folksiness, his being just a regular fellow. Byrne pictured Sandman as too conservative, too concerned with big business, and indifferent to the needs of the people of the state. Sandman's releases painted Byrne as inexperienced, inconsistent, and too liberal. Byrne and Sandman agreed on the difference between them as potential governors: Byrne was likely to be an activist, and Sandman was less likely to use the power of the state government to deal with what he would consider local problems. Of course, these attributes were not the only ones mentioned in the releases, but they were the ones most often stressed. They were the attributes that the campaign organizations wanted the voters to respond to, and therefore they were the attributes they wanted the press to use in their reports.

To say that these attributes were also stressed in the news items based on the releases is to say too much, yet these attributes were not ignored either. Since many of the qualities were stressed in quotations, and since, as noted, such quotations were often among the first parts of releases deleted by editors, there is less emphasis on candidates' attributes in the news stories than in the releases. But despite the reduced emphasis, the images of the candidates in the news stories based on the releases were similar to those in the releases themselves.

For example, the Sandman release announcing the appointment of Mrs. Pearl Bassett as Morris County coordinator for the Sandman campaign included one sentence, a quotation from Bassett, that referred favorably to Sandman's experience: "Throughout his 17 years as a legislator, ten in the New Jersey Senate, and seven in Congress, Congressman Sandman has taken a firm stand in favor of home rule."[23] This quotation also emphasized Sandman's consistency in public stands on important issues. When the *Morristown* (New Jersey) *Daily Record* ran a news story on the item two days later, the quotation was not included.[24] Similarly, the Byrne release announcing the endorsement he received from Republican Morton Howard contained quotations from Howard criticizing Sandman and praising Byrne. Specifically, Howard called Byrne a "man of unquestioned integrity and talent who will become an able Governor."[25] The news item based on this release, which ran in the *Montclair* (New Jersey) *Times* that week, did not include this quotation.[26]

In other instances, however, even though the release was not used in its entirety, the stress on the candidate's favorable attributes did come through. When the American Conservative Union announced its endorsement of Jim Inhofe for the First Congressional District seat from Oklahoma, it devoted most of the release detailing its reasons for opposing the incumbent, Representative James Jones, but it also said that "Inhofe's record in the Oklahoma state legislature shows him to be a principled, consistent conservative."[27] The *Tulsa Tribune* story reporting the endorsement included the favorable reference, although much of the criticism of Jones was deleted.[28] Consider, too, the time when Willy Wright, president of the United Afro-American Association in New Jersey, announced the association's endorsement of Charles Sandman. He contrasted Byrne and Sandman on their political experience and concluded that the latter "has all the political savvy needed."[29] The story in the *Red Bank* (New Jersey) *Register* reporting the endorsement printed the comparison and Wright's conclusion.[30] In a similar instance, the endorsement of Byrne by Louis F. Di Nicola was announced in a release that quoted Di Nicola praising Byrne: "Judge Byrne has the background and the integrity to return government to its desired place of respect."[31] The story in the Salem, New Jersey, *Today's Sunbeam* quoted the sentence just cited, but it did not include the comment by Di Nicola that Sandman was "an extremist who is unqualified" to be governor of New Jersey.[32] In these cases, the desired emphasis on the candidates' favorable qualities came through, even though some criticism of the opposing candidate was omitted. Of course, in those instances where the releases were used verbatim, the criticism came through as well.

But it is not correct to infer from these examples that editors will more readily remove critical remarks than favorable comments from releases. Quite a few critical comments survive. For instance, the July 22, 1973, Byrne release reporting the statement by New Jersey AFL-CIO President Charles Marciante is almost totally an anti-Sandman statement.[33] The *Vineland Times Journal* quoted virtually all of Marciante's critical remarks, leaving out the statement that "Charles Sandman scares" Marciante.[34] Along those same lines is the release announcing the endorsement of Sandman by a group of prominent Democrats, chief of whom was Richard Buggelli. The statement refers to Byrne as "the candidate of far left politics and radical chic"[35] and attempts to tie Byrne to McGovern's ill-fated presidential candidacy of the previous year through their common supporter, Ann Klein. Buggelli referred to the McGovern-Klein-Byrne faction of the state Democratic party, claiming that this faction was both far left and radical. The *Toms River* (New Jersey) *Reporter* story about the endorsement used all of these critical remarks, even though it did not print everything Buggelli said about Byrne and Klein.[36]

Although some attempts to stress favorable attrbutes were successful (and some unsuccessful), it is not true that editors were more likely to let favorable comments go through, nor is it true that either Byrne or Sandman was favored by the treatment their releases received.

The images of the candidates that the voters of New Jersey had available to them, because of the use of candidate news releases by the New Jersey press, were remarkably similar to the pictures they would have gotten had they read all of the releases themselves. The only noteworthy difference is that the total volume of references to Byrne and Sandman's good and bad points in the releases was much greater than in the news stories. The editors did cut the releases before using them, but the trimming pruned away excess, not substance. In communicating their images, the candidates were successful.

The news stories based on the releases, however, did not convey the images of the two candidates as future governors in much detail. To be sure, there was not a great deal of comment on this point in the releases, but there was enough so that reading all of the releases gives one a firm conception of Byrne as a probable activist, and Sandman comes across as a governor reluctant to use his powers in matters that could conceivably be handled by counties or cities. Readers of the news stories had to infer these images from the positions on the issues the candidates took, as reported in the press.

The issues Byrne and Sandman addressed, as discussed in chapter 4—taxation and transportation policies—were treated evenhandedly by the New Jersey press. The question is to what extent the positions the candidates took in the releases were evident in the news items based on those releases. The work here is hampered, because quite a few news stories reported at the same time statements by the candidates that were not in the releases. It is difficult, therefore, to isolate the impact of the releases on the final news items. To the extent that such statements from the releases made it through the editorial process, the releases had an impact.

Byrne's ambiguous stand on the need for new taxes for state government in the releases was accurately reflected in the news items based on those releases. For example, after Governor William T. Cahill announced that the state would finish the fiscal year with a budget surplus of more than $200 million, Byrne issued a short statement in which he said that "as governor, I would not immediately need a new source of revenue to run the state government."[37] The implication was that revenues would be sufficient for state government operations, because of the surplus, for the moment, but not necessarily for the entire four-year gubernatorial term. Byrne kept his options open. The news stories reporting this statement retained the ambiguity. The *Newark* (New Jersey) *Star-Ledger* quoted the entire three-paragraph statement, including the section just cited.[38] More interestingly, the *Hackensack* (New Jersey) *Record,* which paraphrased Byrne's statement, kept the word "immediately" in its report: "Brendan T. Byrne . . . said the surplus meant the new governor would not immediately need new taxes."[39] Neither one of these reports pinned down the Democratic candidate on the need for new taxes sometime during the next four years.

Sandman's campaign press releases tried to picture him as the man "whose opposition to a New Jersey income tax is legend," and although that sentence did not appear in any of the news stories, the press reports based on his releases left no doubt that Sandman opposed an income tax.[40] "I am unalterably opposed to the state income tax,"[41] Sandman declared, and the *Camden* (New Jersey) *Courier-Post* quoted the statement in full.[42] Sandman claimed that he had been fighting a state income tax for twenty years, but Byrne had opposed it for only twenty days.[43] The Trenton, New Jersey, *Trentonian,* while commenting that "both major party candidates have virtually taken the same stance on the income tax, claiming it can be avoided for the foreseeable future," did report Sandman's claim that the difference between his opposition to the tax and Byrne's was that Sandman had been at it so much longer.[44] The *Lambertville,* New Jersey, *Beacon* printed Sandman's release saying that the election "will be a referendum on an income tax" verbatim, except for some omitted paragraphs;[45] it did, however, quote Sandman's firm statement: "I have made my pledge; there will be no state income tax or state-wide property tax during my term as Governor.''[46] It left out Sandman's attempt to reduce the election to one factor: ''if you don't want new state taxes, vote for Charles Sandman.''[47] Voters reading the news stories based on the releases dealing with taxation policies had no doubt where Charles Sandman stood. His clear position in the releases was accurately reflected in the newspaper's treatment of them. Again, however, and this was true of Byrne as well, the volume of references to the candidates' tax policies based on the releases was small compared to the volume available.

The same conclusion is warranted about use of releases dealing with transportation issues. Byrne and Sandman differed in their approaches to the problem of public transportation in New Jersey. Byrne favored having the ''Port Authority of New York and New Jersey operate New Jersey's commuter railroads,'' using federal subsidies and the Port Authority operating surpluses.[48] Byrne's release got comparatively good coverage; five papers wrote stories based on it and on the position paper that accompanied it. ''An agency with net surpluses in excess of $80 million last year should not be permitted to evade its original mandate—to plan and develop a transportation system for the port district,'' Byrne commented, and the statement was picked up by two papers, the *Elizabeth* (New Jersey) *Daily Journal* and the *Trenton* (New Jersey) *Evening Times,* which, however, used the figure $180 million.[49] Byrne's position on the Port Authority's role in New Jersey's commuter-train problems received fair, accurate, and widespread coverage.

Sandman's plan to deal with the same problem, detailed in a release issued five days after Byrne's, got even better press coverage. Nine New Jersey papers dealt with it, and two of them printed the release verbatim. Basically, Sandman's position was to create a ''new transportation authority with far-reaching powers'' to deal with the problems of New Jersey's bankrupt commuter railroads and keep them running.[50] Most of the news accounts based on the release summarized Sandman's position in detail, and some supplied added information, probably based on a speech Sandman gave on the subject. But Sandman's long release announcing the endorsement he received from Philip B. Hoffman, a Port Authority commissioner from New Jersey, which included a long restatement of the transportation proposal, did not fare nearly so well.[51] Only two newspapers picked up the release, the *Red Bank* (New Jersey) *Reg-*

ister and Jersey City's *Jersey Journal.*[52] Neither news item was over four paragraphs long, both short summaries of the facts cited in the release. The *Jersey Journal* spent more time speculating whether Hoffman's endorsement meant that Cahill was moving closer to the Sandman camp than it did talking about either Hoffman or Sandman's transportation plan. It did, however, conclude its story with a quotation from Hoffman, calling Sandman's transportation program "realistic and sound."[53] The *Register's* item included a longer quotation from Hoffman ("In my opinion the mass transportation program proposed by Mr. Sandman is economically sound and makes total sense."[54]) and was totally devoted to the endorsement and the Republican candidate's proposals. In such a short item, however, there was not room to say much.

In the treatment of the transportation-issue releases, Sandman came out on top. His releases were more widely used, and since they followed Byrne's statement, they had the advantage of the last word. The prestige of having the transportation program supported (and the candidate endorsed) by a person of the expertise of Philip Hoffman was another plus—that advantage, however, was not translated into much publicity.

Not all candidates were as successful as these two in getting press coverage of the campaign issues they wanted to stress. For instance, John Anderson issued a number of releases detailing his campaign's progress in qualifying for the ballot in all fifty states, but papers reporting the successes he gained rarely quoted or cited his releases. That progress was evidence for one of the main points Anderson wanted to stress: that his campaign was a viable effort. But since the press had alternative sources of information for those developments (elections officials in various states, courts ruling on the legal aspects, and so forth), they relied very little on Anderson's releases. The result was that the progress was reported without Anderson's interpretation attached to it. The story in the *Kansas City Star* in mid-September 1980 is illustrative. At the end of a story about the Reagan-Anderson debate preparations, the newspaper said, simply, "Meanwhile, Anderson gained two court victories that seemed to ensure that he will be on the general election ballots in Maryland and Minnesota."[55]

Sometimes coverage is a mixed blessing. Take, for instance, the predicament David Boren, then governor of Oklahoma, found himself in during his run for the U.S. Senate in 1978. Boren was publicly labeled a homosexual by one of his opponents for the Democratic nomination, and another opponent sent him a letter asking him to declare whether he was a homosexual or a bisexual and whether he had engaged in homosexual or bisexual activity. Boren responded immediately with a statement calling the charge "utterly ridiculous and categorically untrue."[56] The charge and denial were picked up by three major papers in the state.[57] So far so good, but the charge did not go away, and immediately after the primary election, Boren found it necessary to swear the charge was untrue "with my hand on the Bible which was used in my inaugural ceremony and also in my wedding ceremony."[58] Again, several major papers covered the story, and two ran Boren's sworn affidavit verbatim.[59] Surely, answering the charge in the glare of publicity brought with it disadvantages as well as advantages!

The releases that seemed to be most effective in stimulating news coverage, both for the number of articles generated and for the accuracy of the articles themselves, were some relatively uncontroversial releases. For example, Charles Sandman got good mileage from a release endorsing a referendum for bonds for educational facilities for handicapped children and from a release suggesting that vocational education is a realistic alternative to a college education for a large number of high school graduates. In addition, releases announcing the appearance of then-New York Governor Nelson Rockefeller at Sandman's campaign kick-off dinner got a great deal of press attention. Similarly, Byrne's release announcing the endorsement of a New Jersey's veterans' organization was used by seventeen papers, most of which used it virtually verbatim. Two Byrne releases of human interest only (a girl donates ten cents to the Byrne campaign and a story on Jean Byrne, the candidate's wife) were also used by several papers with no changes. The most widely used Bailey releases were ones that announced that primary opponents now endorsed him, also releases that raised no controversial issues. It is these releases that seem to be most successful in getting into print. The more controversial ones are less likely to be used and more likely to be changed when they are used.

Two reasons for this pattern come to mind. Editors may be more receptive to such noncontroversial releases because they contain less blatant propaganda. Certainly, Sandman wanted to be identified as a supporter of handicapped children, ready to help them where he could, but who doesn't? But Sandman's releases did not make extravagant statements and did not raise extraneous issues. Sandman supported help for handicapped kids, and the readers, who no doubt shared the feeling, probably wanted to know about it. Second, editors of weekly newspapers, many of which have very limited news-gathering budgets, may very well welcome such releases to use as fillers, without having to worry about having to use their scarce resources to develop the other side of a controversial issue.

The newspapers using the releases were, on the whole, conscientious in the way they treated them. Relevant interpretation of the information in the releases, as I suggested in chapter 2, would be necessary to accept the press' treatment of the releases as professional. One might hold two expectations in this regard. One is that the papers would provide background information, where necessary, so that the releases' content would make sense to readers. Another is that, again, where necessary, the news story based on the release indicate that the opponent has been contacted for his side of the controversy. It should be obvious that the former procedure is more likely, since noncontroversial releases would not require comment from the opponent, although they might require background information.

Providing such information was a common practice when the New Jersey press used candidate news releases. About 25 percent of the release uses included background information supplied by the reporter, a total of 266 times out of 968 uses. It seemed that Byrne's releases were much more likely to be fleshed out by background material, since 157 uses of this release received that treatment, compared with only 109 for Sandman's. That difference is probably due in part to the fact that more of Sandman's release uses were verbatim uses, where background information is not supplied. Contacting the opponent was much more rarely done. Slightly more than 3 percent of release uses (34 of 968) indicated that the opposing candidate or a spokesperson had been reached. Twenty-two uses of Sandman's releases included a comment by someone from the Byrne campaign, but replies from Sandman's organization were reported in only 12 uses of Byrne releases. Byrne came out better, since it is somewhat of an advantage not to have the opponent contacted, but the total for both is low. The reason is probably that most charges in the releases were minor. Campaigners save their major accusations and controversial statements that might evoke a response from the opposition for occasions and forums where the exposure is greater.

Jim Inhofe of Oklahoma, however, built much of his campaign on criticism of the incumbent, James Jones, for alleged involvement with the milk fund scandal of the Watergate era, and his releases reflected that emphasis. A number of his releases charged first that Jones was involved and then that Jones was lying in denying his involvement. The various stories in the Tulsa daily press during October when the releases in question were issued all reported a response from Jones to the charges; none was based on an Inhofe release alone. That fact reflects conscientious and impartial treatment of the charges by the press.

But although the press was conscientious in its use of campaign releases, applying its professional standards consistently and impartially, the conclusion that the candidates were successful in using the press as a channel for communicating with voters is inescapable. Although there are some differences among candidates in their success in getting their releases into print, the resulting advantages are not the product of press bias. Even though Sandman had almost all of his endorsement releases used, for example, and Byrne got just slightly over half of his published, there is no evidence that this result came about because the press was biased; in fact, editors may have used proportionately more Sandman endorsements, because they were so much rarer.

The messages in the releases were printed, too. Even though the editors and reporters who control access to print apply standards inconsistent with those of the candidates, it seems that Byrne and Sandman were able to place stories in the press that emphasized the attributes they wanted to stress and that communicated the issue positions they were concerned with. Bailey, too, generated substantial coverage for his releases, and those releases stimulated news stories that presented his message quite well. Part of the success must be attributed to the propaganda devices the candidates used, especially putting crucial messages into quotations and coupling public appearances with press releases. By doing so, the candidates manipulated the press by giving them what they were likely to consider news by their own standards, while the content communicated the messages the candidates wanted to send. Issuing releases in conjunction with public appearances was especially useful for presidential candidates, since so much of media coverage of their campaigns concerned their appearances and comments in public; without the public appearance, the press might very well have ignored the release. But part of the success must also be given to the fact that campaigns themselves are news, and the statements and announcements made in press releases are therefore news as well. Responsible journalists cannot ignore releases as a source of news, and if, in using releases, they help spread propaganda, at the same time they provide their readers with news and with some of the information they need to make up their minds about the candidates. Candidates and the press need each other.

7

DAILIES, WEEKLIES, AND RELEASES

Only the voter who read all of New Jersey's newspapers during the campaign would have been exposed to all of the news stories the Byrne and Sandman releases generated. Those who read less extensively would have been exposed to a selected portion of those releases only, a selection made by the editor of the paper (or papers) they read. The situation is no different for voters in other constituencies; the releases they have a chance to read or read about are also selected by the editors of their local press. Candidate and voter alike are at the mercy of the journalist. Unfortunately, that means the conclusions drawn in the preceding chapter are incomplete. Those conclusions were based on an examination of release use in the aggregate, treating the press not as a collection of individual newspapers, each with its own readership and its own editorial policy, but as a single entity. But to draw conclusions about the success candidates have in reaching individual voters, it is necessary to consider how different newspapers use candidate news releases.

The exposure of individuals to releases depends on which papers they read and on the thoroughness with which they read them. Therefore, precise statements about how many individuals actually read specific news stories stimulated by campaign releases are impossible to make. That requires survey data, data that are unavailable. Instead, I deduced what I could from the information available about the use of releases by newspapers. The conclusion is about *potential* exposure to stories based on releases, not about actual exposure. It is possible to say a great deal about potential exposure. For instance, the voter who regularly reads only the Newton *New*

Jersey Herald is likely to have been exposed to few stories based on campaign press releases. A voter whose regular paper is the *Passaic Herald-News,* on the other hand, will have had the opportunity to read a substantial number of news items based at least in part on candidate releases. Whether the *Passaic Herald-News* reader actually read more of such stories than the *New Jersey Herald* subscriber cannot be determined.

This chapter supports three straightforward propositions. First, Byrne was more successful in obtaining publicity through news releases than Sandman. Second, weekly newspapers are much more likely than daily newspapers to use campaign releases in substantially unaltered formats. Third, many of the differences among newspapers in their use and treatment of releases can be explained by each newspaper's size. The conclusion is that releases generate substantial news coverage, but that there is a trade-off between reaching more voters with a news story based on a reporter-written version of the campaign release and reaching fewer voters with a news story using the release almost verbatim.

One hundred forty-six publications used one or more of the Byrne and Sandman releases; most of them were weekly papers, a total of 107; 2 were college daily papers; and 3 publications appeared monthly. Of the 34 daily newspapers using some of the releases, 5 were published outside the state: the *Easton* (Pennsylvania) *Express;* the *New York Times;* the *New York Daily News;* the *Philadelphia Inquirer;* and the *Philadelphia Evening Bulletin.* The total number of release uses involved, 968, does not represent the total number of news items, since several stories used information from more than one release, but the publications averaged over 6.5 uses each.

That average is much higher than for papers in the Missouri and Indiana congressional races, discussed earlier. Forty-two newspapers used campaign releases issued by Wendell Bailey in 1980, eight of which were daily papers and twenty-three of which were weeklies. (The remaining papers could not be classified from standard reference works). Since these publications used Bailey releases a total of 195 times, each paper averaged only 4.64 uses each. This figure is as high as it is because releases and coverage from both the primary and general election campaigns were considered. Fithian's releases were used by only twenty-one papers for a total of 24 times, an average of 1.14 uses per paper, again covering both primary and general election campaigns. Of course, Fithian issued very few releases, and in both cases, the number of papers in their districts is substantially lower than the number in New Jersey. For these candidates, there were simply not as many newspapers to use their releases.

It is clear from the evidence that readers of some newspapers had the opportunity to read many more stories using press releases than did readers of other newspapers. This fact is not surprising, but the magnitude of the difference between newspapers is startling. The newspaper in New Jersey using the most press releases was the *Newark Star-Ledger,* by far the largest newspaper in the state in circulation, with seventy-nine uses of releases. At the other extreme were forty-four papers, forty-two of them weeklies and two monthlies, each of which used only one press release. The daily with the lowest use of candidate news releases was the *Woodbury* (New Jersey) *Times,* using only two Byrne or Sandman releases; the weekly using the most of these releases was the *Pleasantville* (New Jersey) *Mainland Journal,* which used thirteen releases during the campaign. The range was not so great among papers using the Bailey releases. The daily using the most was the *West Plains* (Missouri) *Daily Quill* with twenty uses of the Bailey releases, and the daily using the fewest was the Pulaski, Missouri, *Daily Fort Gateway Guide.* But several weeklies used substantial numbers of releases, such as the Hermann, Missouri, *Advertiser-Courier* with thirteen uses and the *Washington* (Missouri) *Missourian* with twelve. The difference in potential exposure of readers of different papers to the releases, then, is surprisingly large. It was extremely difficult for the candidates to reach *Woodbury Times* readers, and it proved much easier to get at least some access to the readers of the *Newark Star-Ledger.*

One would expect daily newspapers to have used more candidate press releases than weekly papers, for at least two reasons. Daily newspapers publish five, six, or seven times a week, compared with the once-a-week schedule for weeklies, and they have therefore a corresponding greater capacity for news from all sources, including releases. In addition, dailies, more than weeklies, attempt to provide a relatively complete picture of national and statewide political developments and are thus more receptive to gubernatorial and congressional campaign releases than are weeklies, which, if they cover politics at all, are more concerned with local political news.

Daily newspapers did use more releases than weekly newspapers in the New Jersey campaign. Of the 962 uses of campaign releases, excluding the 6 uses by three monthly publications, 669 or almost

70 percent of them were by daily newspapers. The remaining 293 uses were in the state's weekly press. If a candidate news release was used at all, it was twice as likely to be used by a daily as by a weekly. The mean usage of releases by weeklies was 2.74 releases per paper; for dailies, the figure was 18.08. By contrast, the figure for dailies using Bailey's releases was only 7.75 per paper, and dailies together accounted for only 39.7 percent of the release uses in his district. Weeklies there averaged about 4.1 release uses per paper, higher than the figure for New Jersey weeklies. The difference between New Jersey weeklies and dailies in mean usage virtually disappears when the figures are controlled for frequency of publication. Dividing the dailies' mean usage by the number of times the largest of them publish each week, seven, the result is 2.58, which is directly comparable to the figure for weeklies: the mean number of release uses per publication date. That kind of adjustment to the Bailey figures yields an average of about 1.11 release per publication date, only about one-fourth the average for weeklies.

Weeklies, then, seem to be receptive to releases. Why do weeklies use so many releases from statewide or congressional campaigns? The answer is that the candidates provide quite a few releases that focus attention on localities, either by featuring a local notable appointed to a campaign position or making an endorsement, by the candidate's local appearance, or by stressing a local issue. These releases meet weeklies' needs. Despite the two-to-one edge dailies held in using the Byrne and Sandman releases overall, weeklies used announcements of local campaign appointments, for example, on ten more occasions than did dailies, forty-eight to thirty-eight. Bailey used the propensity of weeklies to publicize local concerns to advantage. His low key, "friends-and-neighbors" campaign avoided the controversies that weeklies also avoid.

The rates at which dailies and weeklies used Byrne's and Sandman's releases, however, were different. Dailies in New Jersey were more likely to use Byrne's releases than Sandman's by a margin of 355 to 314. Since more Sandman releases were used, it follows that Sandman had a large margin over Byrne in uses by weekly papers. The figures here are 179 for Sandman and 114 for Byrne. But Byrne's lead in use of his releases by dailies gave him an edge in total potential exposure to his releases.

That edge is simply the result of the larger circulation of the daily papers that used Byrne's releases. An uncomplicated measure of the potential exposure resulting from the use of a release is to multiply the number of times a release was used by the circulation of the paper using the release (New Jersey circulation alone for out-of-state papers). If, for instance, one paper used one Anderson release, the potential exposure that release would generate would be equal to the circulation of that paper. If that same paper used four Reagan releases, the potential exposure it provided for Reagan releases would be four times the paper's circulation. Comparing totals for each candidate yields an estimate of the success the candidate had in generating publicity through his campaign news releases.

That the estimates are rough at best is apparent; the measure is based on circulation, not readership. It does not take into account the difference in attractiveness various papers may have. The hometown daily, for which the reader pays a monthly subscription fee, is treated the same as the weekly advertising tabloid that is distributed free, and without being ordered, to each resident in the community. Surely, the former paper is more likely to be read than the latter.

Byrne's campaign news releases generated a total of 38,508,523 potential exposures, over 17 percent more than Sandman's total of 32,749,326 potential exposures. These figures are substantial. Consider the cost of television time to reach an equivalent audience, the number of billboards needed to be seen by that many motorists, or the cost of a direct mail campaign to reach that many households. Of course, there is duplication here. These figures do not represent 70,000,000 different readers (particularly not, given the number of people in New Jersey), but the totals are still impressive.

Even more impressive, and at the same time startling, is the number of potential exposures that result from the use of the releases by the New Jersey daily press alone. Byrne's releases generated almost 38.0 million potential exposures in daily newspapers, leaving a comparatively paltry 900,000 or so exposures distributed among the state's weekly papers. Sandman's figures are comparable. He obtained 31.0 million such exposures from daily papers, compared with about 1.3 million potential exposures in weeklies. Sandman's edge in the use of releases by weekly papers becomes inconsequential in comparison to the tremendous total of potential exposures provided by the state's daily papers.

Since other candidates issued many fewer releases, and since fewer and smaller papers serve some other constituencies, these impressive totals of potential exposures are not easily matched.

Bailey, for instance, generated over a million potential exposures with his news releases, two-thirds of which came from daily papers. Fithian, issuing so few releases, obtained just over a quarter million potential exposures, of which 90 percent came from daily papers. These figures, however, have to be considered in context. If one campaign release is used once by the *Los Angeles Times,* for instance, just over a million potential exposures are generated. A candidate running for office in a sparsely populated rural area needs to reach the voters through the relatively small home-town papers, many of them weeklies, that they read. But a candidate running for statewide office in a state with at least one large metropolitan area can easily reach several times the number of voters with only a couple of news releases picked up by the daily paper serving the metropolis.

It is interesting to compare the ten papers that gave Sandman and Byrne the most potential exposures from their campaign releases. The entire two lists are presented as table 7.1. Seven papers appear on both lists, headed by the *Newark Star-Ledger,* in each case providing the most exposures. Three out-of-state papers—the two New York papers and the *Philadelphia Evening Bulletin*—are on both lists, indicating that these papers were important to the candidates in reaching voters. Only the *Star-Ledger,* the *Hackensack*

Table 7.1: Newspapers Providing the Most Potential Exposures from Releases, by Candidate

BYRNE		SANDMAN	
Newspaper	Potential Exposures	Newspaper	Potential Exposures
Newark Star-Ledger	14,749,636	*Newark Star-Ledger*	11,732,665
Hackensack Record	3,022,260	*Hackensack Record*	2,417,808
New York Times	2,587,740	*New York Daily News*	2,073,400
Trenton Evening Times	2,301,390	*Trenton Evening Times*	1,917,825
Passaic Herald-News	1,962,994	*New York Times*	1,522,200
New York Daily News	1,481,000	*Atlantic City Press*	1,486,562
Trenton *Trentonian*	1,294,898	*Camden Courier-Post*	1,227,740
Elizabeth Daily Journal	1,274,140	*Philadelphia Bulletin*	1,146,544
Philadelphia Bulletin	1,146,544	*Union City Dispatch*	991,260
Asbury Park Press	1,023,432	*Passaic Herald-News*	981,497

Source: Computed from clippings supplied by Representative Sandman's office.

Record, and the *Trenton Evening Times* generated more total exposures (both candidates combined) than did the *New York Times,* for instance. Three papers appearing on the Sandman list that did not make the Byrne top ten are published in areas where Sandman had greater support. Atlantic City is the largest city in his congressional district, Camden is also in southern New Jersey, and the *Union City Dispatch* is in the heart of Hudson County, where Byrne was relatively weak. On the other hand, the three papers on the Byrne list that did not appear on Sandman's serve an area stretching across the center of New Jersey—Trenton, Elizabeth, and Asbury Park—an area where Byrne was stronger than Sandman.

All of these papers are dailies. In Bailey's district, however, several of the papers that yielded him the most potential exposures from his campaign releases were weeklies. Of course, fewer dailies were in his district, but even so the third and sixth positions on his list of most important exposures were held by weeklies. Third was the *Washington* (Missouri) *Missourian,* and sixth was the Hermann, Missouri, *Advertiser-Courier.* Again, for Bailey, weeklies were relatively more important than they were for other candidates.

Why do some papers use more releases than others? Several explanations are possible. Size of the paper seems to have a lot to do with it, at least for dailies. A simple correlation between circulation and the number of times a paper used releases yielded a coefficient of .485 for daily papers and -.079 for weekly papers in New Jersey. The correlation for use of Byrne releases produced values of .484 and -.023; the corresponding values for the use of Sandman's releases were .442 and -.086. The negative correlation between use and circulation for weeklies should not be disturbing. The value themselves are small enough to indicate that there is virtually no relationship between the two variables. But for daily papers, the correlation coefficient is surprisingly strong. Almost 25 percent of the variance in use of the releases can be accounted for by circulation alone. There is much less difference in the correlation coefficients for use of the Bailey releases. The association between circulation and use of releases by dailies is .432, comparable to the New Jersey figures, but the association between circulation and use of releases by weeklies is a relatively robust .356.

One implication of this result for dailies in New Jersey needs to be emphasized. Not only are larger dailies more likely to use releases than are smaller dailies, but when they use them, the candidates reach more readers. The value to the candidate of having a paper such as the *Trenton Evening Times,* with a circulation of 76,713 in 1973, use a campaign news release rather than, say, the Willingboro *Burlington County Times,* with a circulation of 35,308 in 1973, is substantial enough. But when it is clear that the *Evening Times* is more likely to use a release in the first place, the candidate has an added incentive to tailor his releases to the needs of the larger papers. If the smaller papers use them, too, that will be welcome, but the larger papers provide markedly better publicity returns for the effort expended.

A paper's political affiliation may also explain why it used more of one candidate's releases than another's. Unfortunately, for an analysis of such a relationship, few New Jersey papers explicitly avow a preference for one party. That is a national pattern as well; most of the large metropolitan dailies call themselves politically independent. In New Jersey, one weekly and one daily identified themselves with the Democratic party, and four weeklies and no dailies indicated a preference for the Republicans. Five weeklies and four dailies called themselves Independent Republican, and the other publications claimed to be politically independent. In Bailey's district, five weeklies are Republican, and two dailies and eight weeklies are Democratic, the rest calling themselves Independent. The data are therefore sketchy.

The Democratic weekly in New Jersey used one Byrne release and no Sandman releases, which is in line with expectations, but the daily that called itself Democratic, the *Union City Dispatch,* used thirteen Byrne releases to eighteen of Sandman's. One cannot put too much reliance on evidence from only one paper, however. There are more Republican-inclined papers to work with if we combine the straight Republican press with the Independent Republicans. The four dailies in this classification used sixteen Byrne releases and fifteen Sandman releases, splitting almost exactly down the middle. The nine weeklies, however, fell squarely into the Sandman column, using fifteen of his releases among them and only three of Byrne's. But of the four sets of data, only the set involving weekly Republican papers showed a use of releases consistent with the hypothesis that party affiliation helps account for release use.

The Bailey data are no clearer. The Democratic papers were as likely to use many Bailey releases as they were to use fewer, but the Republican papers were much more likely to use only a few

Bailey releases. The Democratic papers gave the Republican Bailey, then, somewhat more publicity than did the avowedly Republican papers.

Perhaps, however, the endorsement the paper plans to make in the campaign influences the choices involved in using releases. Again, the data are few.[1] Of six weeklies endorsing a candidate for governor of New Jersey and using at least one candidate news release, only one endorsed Sandman, and that paper used one release from both candidates. The other five weeklies used five of Byrne's releases but twelve Sandman releases, despite the Byrne endorsement. All relevant dailies endorsing a candidate suggested that their readers vote for Byrne, and Byrne's releases were substantially more likely to be used, 161 uses versus 108 uses of Sandman's releases. Of the 269 uses of campaign releases by dailies that endorsed a gubernatorial candidate, Byrne's releases accounted for 59.9 percent of them; of the 400 uses by dailies that did not endorse a candidate, Byrne's releases were involved only 48.5 percent of the time. It should be noted that the *Newark Star-Ledger* did not endorse a candidate in 1973; its edge of 44 to 35 uses for Byrne helps to raise Byrne's percentage to 48.5.

But since no dailies endorsed Sandman, and since so few weeklies endorsed either candidate, it is difficult to conclude that the use of releases by the newspapers involved is influenced by their endorsement. The argument would be difficult to make in any case, since an endorsement is rarely made early in the campaign. Before the endorsement is made, the editors are called upon to decide how to use specific releases the candidates have submitted. One might even argue that editors impressed by the quality of the releases sent to them may be more likely to endorse such an efficient candidate. In that case, releases worthy enough to be used in their own right would influence the endorsement, rather than the endorsement influencing the use and treatment of the releases.

In chapter 5, I reported that some editors said that whether candidates advertised with their papers influenced their decisions to use releases.[2] Placing such advertising is a clear indication to the editor that the candidate considers the paper's readers important to his campaign; editors are presumably more willing to use a candidate's releases in such a situation. The presupposition is, of course, that an editor who makes the decisions about using a candidate's releases is in a position to know what advertising, if any, the candidate has placed with his paper. We would not expect a city editor on a large paper such as the *Houston Post* to have that kind of information; therefore, if there is to be any relationship between advertising in a paper and its use of a candidate's releases, it is likely to be modest at best. Because many weeklies are virtually one-person operations as far as editing and publishing are concerned, weeklies are probably more likely to reflect a relationship between using releases and advertising.

No records for placement of advertising in newspapers by the Byrne campaign are available. The reports it filed with the New Jersey election commissioner indicate advertising expenditures through agencies only, with no breakdown on how the advertising money was distributed among various media. The Sandman reports are a little more detailed. Although they too indicate disbursements to advertising agencies for placing advertisements, the reports include separate listings for a number of papers. Thirteen of these publications also used campaign press releases. Again, the data are skimpy.

Three dailies received Sandman advertising money: the Willingboro *Burlington County Times,* the *Atlantic City Press,* and the New Brunswick *Home News.* The *Home News* used more Byrne releases than Sandman releases, and by a wide margin, eight to two, but the *Times* and *Press* used more Sandman releases, seven of eleven for the *Times* and twenty-two of thirty-one for the *Press.* Sandman placed advertising in nine weeklies that also used either Byrne or Sandman campaign releases. Overall, he received fifteen of twenty-three uses from these papers, but only four papers gave him an edge over Byrne. The last publication was a monthly that used one release, and it happened to be a Sandman release.

The limitations of these data should be clear: we do not have any information about the placement of Byrne advertisements. It may be that Byrne placed as much, if not more, advertising in each of these papers as did Sandman. The fact that Sandman obtained forty-seven of seventy-six release uses involved would then be due to factors other than advertising. On the surface, however, the evidence does not contradict the expectation that placing advertisements will lead to editors using a candidate's releases.

Brendan Byrne, Charles Sandman, and Wendell Bailey, then, generated quite a bit of publicity for their campaign with news releases, and of the three, Byrne was probably most successful.

It can be expected that candidates who conscientiously issue well-prepared releases would experience correspondingly successful responses from editors. Such candidates may want more specific information about the characteristics of releases that successfully generate campaign coverage.

Recall that in the preceding chapter we obtained a multiple correlation of .308 for the use of releases and length, campaign week, and newsworthiness for both New Jersey candidates' releases combined. When the release uses are divided into two categories, use by weeklies and use by dailies, these three factors predict use by releases somewhat better for dailies ($R = .403$) but somewhat less accurately for weeklies ($R = .104$). The difference between the two types of papers is striking. These factors explain a substantial portion of the variance for daily papers but virtually none of it for weeklies.

It is reassuring to note that daily newspapers seem to respond to a release's newsworthiness; after all, that is what editors said they looked for in releases in their responses to the questionnaires. The situation for weekly editors is different, since they indicated that local interest or relevance is important to them, and the index does not include a measure of local interest. There is an incentive, then, for campaigners to make their releases newsworthy; they are then definitely more likely to be used by dailies, and releases used by dailies provide a substantial amount of publicity. Byrne did well on this score, compared to Sandman.

Sandman, however, did better in the way the press treated his releases. Since the content of the releases is comprised of messages and images the candidate wants to convey to potential voters, treatment of the releases that retain substantial portions of the original wording increases the likelihood that the candidate's messages will reach the voters. Verbatim use, or verbatim use with paragraphs deleted, either at the end or in the middle of the release, are the most desirable treatments from the candidate's perspective; summaries, rewritings, and "other" treatments may retain little of the content the candidates are concerned with communicating. Sandman, as we saw in the previous chapter, had more of his releases used in one of the first three ways than did Byrne.

The reason is simply that weeklies tend to give campaign press releases more favorable treatment than do dailies, and weeklies used more Sandman releases than Byrne releases. As a matter of fact, dailies in New Jersey used releases verbatim only 33 times, compared with 113 times for weeklies. In Bailey's campaign, dailies used releases verbatim only four times, but weeklies did so 58 times. In addition, there were 13 more verbatim uses with paragraphs deleted. To put the New Jersey figures differently, 4.9 percent of all uses by dailies were verbatim uses, and 38.6 percent of all uses by weeklies were verbatim. If we combine the three variations of verbatim use, only 13.2 percent of all release uses by dailies in New Jersey were of these kinds, and almost three-fourths or 72 percent of release uses by weeklies were. See table 7.2.

Table 7.2: Treatment of Releases by Weekly and Daily New Jersey Newspapers

TREATMENTS	VERBATIM OR VERBATIM WITH PARAGRAPHS DROPPED	SUMMARIES, REWRITES, OR "OTHER" TREATMENTS	TOTAL
Weeklies	211	82	293
Dailies	88	581	669

Source: Computed from clippings supplied by Representative Sandman's office.
Note: X^2_y = 326.81, 1 df, $p <$ .001, V = .504.

Sandman's releases were published verbatim by weekly newspapers more often than were Byrne's, 66 times compared with 47 times. Dailies, however, printed eighteen of Byrne's releases verbatim, but only fifteen of Sandman's. Combining the first three treatments indicates that even dailies used Sandman's releases more faithfully to their content than Byrne's. In fact, Sandman's releases were used by weeklies either verbatim or verbatim with paragraphs deleted 136 times, compared with only 75 times for Byrne. Dailies made 54 such uses of Sandman's releases, compared with 34 for Byrne. Because so many more of Sandman's releases were used by weeklies than were Byrne's, more Sandman releases were treated in one of the last three ways, 43, than were Byrne's, 39, although in percentage terms, there were more uses of Byrne's releases receiving such treatment (34.2 percent) than Sandman's (24.0 percent).

For every subject category, weeklies used releases verbatim or nearly so the majority of the time, and that is true for Bailey as well as for Byrne and Sandman individually. But in no instance did dailies use candidate releases verbatim or verbatim with paragraphs deleted more often than they did in other ways. In fact, almost exactly one-third of all uses of releases by the New Jersey daily press involved someone rewriting the release into an appropriate news item. Another 30 percent of the uses received an "other" treatment. These results are very much in line with the Bailey results, with the use of the Anderson and Reagan releases in the nation's major papers, and with the use of the Inhofe and Boren releases in the Oklahoma daily press. They are consistent, also, with the responses editors of dailies gave in the questionnaires. They indicated that releases almost always needed to be rewritten, and they said so more often than editors of weekly papers. It follows that the influence that editors of daily papers exert over the content of campaign press releases is potentially greater than that wielded by weekly editors.

One may ask why some newspapers treat releases more favorable to the candidate than others; that is, why are some papers more likely to run releases with few if any changes? It is possible that the size of the newspaper may have something to do with it. Consider, for instance, the major metropolitan daily, with a large reportorial staff and an image of itself as the "paper of record." It would be likely to try to inform its readers of as many developments as possible. But if it views itself as an independent journalistic enterprise with its own perspective and its professional reputation to maintain, it would be unlikely to use releases verbatim. Instead, one would expect such a paper to summarize several releases in one story or to have a reporter rewrite a release to emphasize what the editor thinks is the main news in the release.

A smaller daily, on the other hand, may be limited in the resources that it can commit to covering the news for its readers. It would still, however, want to keep its readers abreast of the current developments within those limits. The subjects that such a daily would try to cover would necessarily be more limited; they would center more on topics of local interest, but state and national affairs would also be followed. One would expect such a daily to assign a reporter to cover a candidate's personal appearance in the area or to rewrite a release with few changes. Using a release with general rather than local interest in that way may be better than not covering the development at all, when the time of the editors cannot be spared to rework the material.

In addition, some weeklies see their mission as one of providing a forum for local candidates to reach local voters. The difference between the paper as a forum and as a channel should be clear:

when a paper acts as a forum, it opens its columns to the candidate; when it acts as a channel, it tells its readers about the candidate and his messages. For instance, the editor of the *Clinch Valley Times* of St. Paul, Virginia, said:

In county and local elections, we discourage press releases from the candidates or their managers. Instead, we solicit from *each* candidate for each post a statement of why he or she wishes to be elected (or re-elected), and present this information, *clearly* designated as coming from the candidates. . . . . These comments were *solicited* by us and printed as a public service (no fee charged the candidates). *All* candidates are included, whether or not they have advertised with us.[3]

She enclosed a copy of the November 1, 1979, page printing such candidate statements. When editors view the function of their newspaper in the community in this light, one would expect a great deal less editing and rewriting of the statements submitted by campaigners.

If the difference between weeklies and dailies is due in part to their relative sizes, it is worthwhile to see whether newspaper size within these categories is related to treatment of releases. To do so, it is necessary to divide the newspapers that used the New Jersey releases into categories by circulation. (Unfortunately, there was not enough variation in circulation among papers covering the Bailey campaign to draw any conclusions in this way.) There were 107 weekly newspapers involved. Papers with a circulation of four thousand or less were defined as "small," those with circulations between four thousand and eight thousand as "medium," and weeklies with circulations over eight thousand as "large." There were 34, 41, and 32 papers in these three categories, respectively. For dailies, the dividing line between the two circulation categories I used was fifty thousand. The five out-of-state papers were included, as were the college dailies. There were 17 "small" dailies and 19 "large" dailies. Three monthly publications that used candidate releases were not included in the analysis.

The rate at which large dailies used campaign news releases was markedly higher than the rate for small dailies. The large papers used releases 506 times, for an average of over 26 uses per paper; the small dailies, however, had only 163 release uses, averaging under 10 per paper. The differences among weeklies were not so great. Large- and medium-size weeklies used releases at virtually the same rate, an average of just over 2.9 times each; small weeklies used releases on the average about 2.2 times each. Four of these five sets of newspapers used more Sandman releases than Byrne releases; the exception was the large dailies, where Byrne had a 275 to 231 lead. But even the small dailies used more Sandman releases than Byrne releases, although just barely, 83 to 80. Small and large weeklies used almost twice as many Sandman releases as Byrne's, but medium-size weeklies were a little more evenly split, with 69 Sandman uses to 54 Byrne uses.

There is little difference between large and small dailies in their choice of releases to use by release category. Large dailies tended to use a slightly higher percentage of releases from the candidate-statement category than did small dailies, and small dailies used larger proportions of campaign-appointment announcements than did large dailies. The percentages for the other three categories were virtually identical.

That similarity between large and small dailies contrasts sharply with the difference in the way they used the releases. Only twenty-eight uses by large dailies consisted of verbatim treatments or one of the two variations, but there were sixty such uses among the small dailies. The relationship between circulation and release treatment was moderate: $V = .369$ ($X^2_y = 102.85$, 1 df, $p < .001$). The difference calls to mind the difference between dailies and weeklies on the same point. The evidence seems to suggest that smaller dailies treat releases as weeklies do. A test of that hypothesis forces us to reject it. Weeklies and small dailies treat releases differently—the hypothesis that they treat releases differently would be *accepted* at the .001 level of confidence, a strong reason to reject the contrary hypothesis, indeed. That would suggest that smaller dailies fit between large dailies and weeklies in their treatment of candidate news releases.

The distribution of release uses among the four subject matter categories by large and small dailies for each of the candidates is similar, but the treatment accorded Sandman's releases by small dailies was more favorable to him than the treatment given Byrne's releases. Almost twice the number of Sandman releases were printed verbatim or verbatim with paragraphs deleted than Byrne releases. Sandman had thirty-nine such uses, and Byrne received only twenty-one from small dailies. For large dailies, however, there is virtually no difference between the candidates. Sandman's releases were used verbatim or nearly so fifteen times by large dailies, compared with thirteen times for Byrne's releases. More favorable treatments of these releases were accorded by small dailies. Circulation does make a difference.

There are few differences among the three classes of weeklies in their use of releases, either in the distribution of the uses among the subject categories or in the way the releases were treated once used. Each category of weeklies, for instance, had about one-third of their uses in the candidate-statement category. Approximately two-thirds of all treatments were verbatim, verbatim with end paragraphs dropped, or verbatim with middle paragraphs deleted. Neither are there important differences among these papers in the way they used releases from each candidate. To be sure, each class of papers was more likely to use Sandman's candidate statements than Byrne's, and they were more likely to use Byrne's endorsements than Sandman's, but Sandman issued more candidate statements in the first place and Byrne sent out quite a few more endorsements. As far as treatment of the releases was concerned, Sandman's releases were in each case somewhat more likely to be used verbatim or nearly so, but the margins are not large. In effect, Sandman's advantage over Byrne in the use of his releases by weekly newspapers is the result basically of the number used, but not of the categories of releases used or the way in which the releases were treated.

At least for dailies, then, the papers that used releases more often, circulation accounts for much of the variation in their treatment of the releases. One might even conclude that three types of newspapers use releases: large dailies, small dailies, and weeklies. The differences between large and small dailies are as important and as substantial as the differences between dailies and weeklies. But differences among weeklies in circulation are not reflected in different treatments of campaign releases.

Given the predilection of many papers to use releases about local developments and local personalities, it was unfortunate for Sandman that he was from southern New Jersey. The largest papers in his state are in northern New Jersey, and each candidate had an edge in the number of releases used by papers in his half of the state.[4] In the southern counties, Sandman had almost twice as many releases used as did Byrne, 172 to 87, and in the north, their positions were reversed, with Byrne leading 329 to 276.

The results in this chapter underscore the difficulty in conducting an issue-oriented campaign through news releases. Releases that are used verbatim are less likely to reach many voters, but releases that may reach a large segment of the electorate are likely to be used in markedly different formats. That is not to say that dailies never use releases verbatim; short statements on important topics may be used essentially as prepared by the candidate, although they may not be given a separate news story. Even dailies need to fill the gaps between their "important" news stories and the advertising—a well-written, concise release may be chosen for such slots. But if an explanation of a position or the presentation of a proposal is involved, press releases are only somewhat effective.

If, on the other hand, the purpose is to build name recognition and to develop an image, candidate releases work well. Byrne, probably more than Sandman, was successful in keeping his name in the press for the entire campaign, a tactic more important to Byrne, because he was so much less well known than the congressman from Cape May. Since he was less well known, he had a better opportunity to build the image he wanted to convey. Sandman had faced the frustrating task of developing an image that could attract a majority of voters in the face of a preexisting public awareness of him that was less than entirely favorable. Mike Andrews, Jim Inhofe, and Mike Antonovich, whose releases were described earlier, took similar tacks in their image-building attempts. They called attention to their incumbent opponents' negative traits and contrasted those traits to their own favorable characteristics. The use made of such releases by major dailies, largely rewrites and summaries, as well as "other" treatments, kept candidates' names in the news, and the contrast with the incumbent helped present the desired image. For these kinds of efforts, candidate news releases are a useful communication device.

A VIABLE CAMPAIGN
TECHNIQUE

The quality of the choices voters make depends to a great extent on the quality and the quantity of the information they obtain. One cannot expect them to choose among candidates or parties on the basis of the likely impact on the voters' futures if voters cannot obtain reliable information on that score. Neither can one expect voters to make such rational choices if the information made available to them about parties, candidates, and issues is misleading.[1] Candidates are major sources of campaign information, but since their fortunes are directly tied up with election outcomes, they do not conduct campaigns so that voters will be able to choose the best possible candidate, but so that they will be the voters' choice. Because of the personal stake candidates have, the information they provide is carefully chosen to influence the electorate's choice. Although it is possible that such information may be reliable and helpful to voters, it is equally possible that it may be misleading.[2] (One incumbent suffering from charges made by his opponent on a radio commercial commented that "truth has never been a requirement" for campaign advertisements.[3]) The crux of the problem is that it is often impossible for the ordinary voter to recognize whether a particular statement by a candidate is reasonable and consistent with his previous record. Campaigns, in other words, provide candidates opportunities to mislead as well as to inform voters. The result is a deluge of propaganda.

Much of the communication between candidates and voters runs through various intermediaries, such as television, party workers, billboards, and newspapers.[4] But media such as the press do not allow all communication from candidates to voters to pass through undisturbed. In that sense, they are not facilitators but selective transmitters, passing on only portions of the tremendous number of messages that could be communicated. The standards that journalists use to distinguish messages worth sending from the others are crucial, because one set of standards will benefit one communicator, and another set will benefit others. Leon Sigal, for instance, reported that the criteria news people used in the 1976 presidential campaign benefited "outsiders" in the contests for presidential nominations against "Washingtonians."[5] In general, the standards journalists use center on their conceptions of what constitutes news.

In reporting newsworthy events, reporters adopt an "objective" perspective, one supposedly free of judgments in favor of or against the development of statements being reported. That raises the central problem with which this study has been concerned: Can candidate news releases—devices campaigners use to send messages to voters that may or may not be factually reliable or misleading through media such as newspapers that hold to standards calling on them to reject such propaganda—be effective campaign communication vehicles? The answer is yes.

Candidate news releases are, of course, only part of a larger effort by candidates to communicate with voters; they supplement, but do not replace, other means. Both Sandman and Byrne issued substantial numbers of releases, 194 by Sandman and 179 by Byrne, indicating that they thought the effort worthwhile. Even presidential candidates such as Reagan and Anderson, running campaigns traditionally thought of as centering on the electronic media, distributed significant numbers of releases as well. That these releases were an integral part of the entire campaign is shown by some simple facts—the rate at which releases are issued reflects closely the tempo of the entire campaign. Byrne, for example, started more quickly and Sandman waited until September before he embarked on a strenuous public campaign. The distribution of releases among subjects mirrors the emphasis that Sandman, for instance, put on local campaign organizations and his own statements and that Byrne put on endorsements, especially from Republicans. Inhofe's releases reflected accurately his strategy to run a campaign to put his opponent on the defensive, a strategy he consistently carried out. At the same time, the stress releases place on the images the candidates wanted to evoke was consistent with the emphasis the rest of the campaign placed on them.[6]

Campaigners use two techniques to maximize the chances that the press will use their releases. They make them newsworthy and disguise the propaganda in them. The newsworthiness index developed in chapter 3, however, did not point out many releases with high scores. Most releases are not very interesting.[7] Propaganda devices, designed to increase the likelihood that the release's content would reach newspaper readers, are widely used. In effect, candidates use journalists' standards of objectivity and impartiality to manipulate the perceptions of news people and their reactions to the releases.[8]

Since the news release is at best a secondary method of reaching voters, candidates reserve announcements of surprising and important developments for other methods. (In any case, the press is not going to be satisfied with releases as the only source of information on such occurrences.) Although they serve limited purposes, then, releases are still valuable tools for campaigners. They are excellent means to keep the candidate's name in the news and to build his image. More issue-oriented purposes are better met through other means of reaching voters. The reason is simply the control the press has over the content of the final news story. There is no guarantee that specific information will get into print, and therefore candidates would be wise to use releases for purposes that do not depend on specific facts. Discussion of issues is better saved for forums where candidates have more control over the content. Although a number of candidates whose releases were examined here discussed a number of issues, most notably Arlen Specter, most emphasized image building and name recognition over issues.

Editors in this study differed in their reactions to releases generally and in their judgment of their usefulness and adequacy specifically. They thought that the releases did not meet their standards of good journalism and that they attempted to stimulate news coverage whether there was any news or not. Yet a substantial number of editors said that they use some campaign releases, and this study has shown that a significant number of news releases are used in some way at least once by some newspapers during a campaign. One would expect, therefore, that editors distinguish between usable and unusable releases on criteria consistent with their explicit standards of newsworthiness.

The index of newsworthiness was a disappointment in this regard. The index had only a slight relationship to the use of releases by itself. In conjunction with the length of the release and the week in which it was issued, the association strengthened. But the low correlation between newsworthiness and release use needs to be discussed.

One major possibility is that the index itself is faulty. No doubt there are important weaknesses, the chief of which is the impossibility of taking into account a crucial determinant of newsworthiness according to editors responding to surveys: local interest. To take local interest into the index, one would need a separate measure of newsworthiness for each of the potential users of the release, and computations of relationships would become complex. Furthermore, the index did not weigh the components. It is clear from the multiple regression reported in chapter 6, however, that the components were not equally important in predicting release use. In a sense, using the components in a multiple regression replaces the index itself. Each component can then contribute as much toward explaining release use as it can.

Another possibility is that the index, although not fully reliable, presents a reasonable picture of the relationship between the newsworthiness of releases and their use. Releases can be used as fillers, making their value as news irrelevant. In addition, releases can provide additional information to flesh out other news stories, and the news value of the release would be only a marginal consideration. The result could be the product, too, of a lack of professionalism among the press. "Too many newspapers," James M. Perry said, "believe it is enough to take press releases from the candidates, write a headline, and toss them into the hopper."[9] If that is the case with the press, it is a significant conclusion. If the use of releases is virtually unrelated to their newsworthiness, there is quite a gap between the statements of editors and their actual practices. David Ostroff noted a similar disparity in television news coverage. His data "point to some differences between the behavior of the local television news organizations and that which has been reported about the networks' coverage of Presidential campaigns."[10]

The gap is smaller for daily editors. The relationship between newsworthiness and use by dailies is a little higher, although not large by any standard. For weeklies, whose editors were less likely to mention newsworthiness as a reason for using releases, the association was smaller. Since most editors of daily papers have greater resources, especially reporters, to deal with releases, one should not be surprised to see a stronger relationship than among weeklies. Where greater professional resources are available, professional standards are more consistently applied.

If the index, although less than perfect, presents a reasonable picture of what the press actually does with candidate news releases, the index should be related, too, to the way in which the releases were actually treated. The results reported in chapter 6 support this expectation. Newsworthy releases were more likely to be accorded a treatment that required a reporter or an editor to change the format and the language of the release. Less newsworthy releases were more likely to be used verbatim or nearly so. These releases were, one might suppose, not worth the editor's time.

The index, then, helps more to distinguish the way in which releases will be treated than in which releases will be used in the first place. The lack of association between the index and release use indicates that the index's components together do not account for variations in use of releases. A different weighting of the components may better explain use of releases.

The way in which the releases are used suggests that the candidates were wise in stressing image building and name recognition in their releases, for too little discussion of the issues (in volume) was available to newspaper readers to make much impact. Candidates, of course, do not build images on a blank slate—their existing images limit their flexibility—but the attributes they emphasize are in large part determined by their evaluations of the contemporary political mood. A few attributes can be emphasized in a campaign, and releases can do that job well. The propaganda devices help. A substantial number of quotations from releases, quotations most often concerned with the candidate's image, survive. In addition, the sheer number of releases used kept the candidates' names in front of the public, even when the releases were merely summarized. In those instances, the essential propaganda that reached the news story was often no more than "C is a candidate for Congress," but even that message is significant, since it can reinforce the candidate's identification with voters.

One further point needs to be made about the use of releases by the press: Rarely did the news stories identify the candidate as the source. Although Mike McCarvile, who ran Jim Inhofe's campaign, said he "can always tell a political release," it is unlikely that the average reader can.[11] If one did not have a copy of the release available, one might not be able to tell that the story was not the result of the reporter's own curiosity, diligence, and investigation. The advantage for candidates, of course, is that the reader is not aware that he is reading candidate-inspired material. To the voter, the story is simply one among many. The obsession with objectivity among reporters, of which readers are dimly aware ("It must be true—I saw it in the paper"), helps the candidate immensely. Material that a voter otherwise would not read or would read with skepticism he reads more readily in the newspaper and, the candidates hope, with a more receptive mind. To be able to cloak propaganda in the newspapers' mystique of objectivity is one of the great advantages of candidate news releases.

The New Jersey press did a decent job of treating the Sandman and Byrne releases. There was no evidence of favoritism because of the papers' party affiliation, because of advertising placed by the candidates, or because of the endorsements the papers made or planned to make. More importantly, the treatment the press there and elsewhere give releases is consistent with editors' explicit statements about releases and with what students of journalism have learned about the news-gathering process. The distinction between dailies and weeklies is, however, crucial; not only do editors of these two types of papers react differently to campaign releases, they explicitly adhere to different standards as well. A further distinction between editors of large dailies and small dailies is necessary. Editors of small dailies are more likely to use releases verbatim, for example, than editors of large dailies, but less likely than editors of weeklies. There are, then, three types of papers in terms of their use and treatment of releases.

How much of this candidate-generated news coverage actually makes an impact on potential voters is difficult to determine. It depends, among other things, on which papers they read, how thoroughly they read them, and to what other sources of information they have access. Surely, one story based on a release is not going to be enough to persuade a rock-ribbed Republican to vote for a Democrat. An Independent is also not very likely to be swayed only on the basis of release-inspired news; for one thing, the paper he reads may have had virtually an equal number of releases used from each of the candidates.

But as part of an ongoing campaign reaching voters from many directions, campaign releases may stimulate coverage consistent with themes and images stressed by other methods of communication. In that case, it is conceivable that the believability of a news story may push a wavering voter in the right direction or solidify a voter who may have doubts about the candidate he is supporting.

Repeated stress on themes is necessary for a voter to become aware of and react to a candidate's campaign. When a voter has come into contact with such themes through media he does not fully trust, he may very well be more receptive to the campaign and to think that the candidate is truthful in his advertising when the themes are echoed by news stories.

Of course, for a campaign technique to have its maximum effect on a voter, it must catch him when he is in the process of deciding for whom to vote. Before that time, news items based on releases may make him aware of the candidate and after that time such news may solidify his choice, but the impact is likely to be greatest when he is making up his mind and is therefore receptive to campaign information. Garrett O'Keefe suggests that a voter may look to the media for such information when he is ready to choose:

Individuals may rely on and react to mass communications differently when they know that they need to arrive at a decision and act upon it by a certain time (Election Day) than when, say, they perform in the more flexible roles of product consumers or entertainment seekers vis-a-vis mass media.[12]

Since voters make up their minds at different times, candidates feel compelled to offer propaganda on their behalf throughout the campaign. One would think that news stories that regularly summarize the candidates' qualifications and positions on campaign issues, say, once a week, would perform a valuable service to voters making up their minds. Unfortunately, such stories are rare, most often coming in the last week or so of the campaign, because after several weeks the stories would become repetitious and would therefore no longer be news. But a voter may require an overview of the campaign, not the latest developments, when he is making up his mind. Candidates seem to recognize the need for such stories, but the press reacts negatively to releases filled with such material: not enough hard news.

If voters read all of the news items based on releases and all of the releases themselves, those that were used as well as those that were not, the picture they would get of the candidates based on the news stories would be similar to the one they would get from the releases directly. The point is worth emphasizing; it is established by the use of the Boren releases, the Inhofe releases, the Bailey and

Fithian releases, the Antonovich, Anderson, and Reagan releases, as well as by the use the New Jersey press made of the Byrne and Sandman releases. Neither the selection of releases from among those issues nor the treatment of those releases by the press seriously altered the images the candidates portrayed during the campaign.

The difference between the releases and the news stories, as far as the voters are concerned, is that the news stories place less emphasis on every attribute and issue the candidates try to stress. Byrne's integrity was mentioned in the stories based on his releases, but not as often as in his releases. Sandman's position on income taxes was reported, but the releases emphasized his opposition much more frequently. Both candidates and voters suffered from this treatment. Voters did not get the information about the position of the candidates on the issues available to them as often as some might have wanted, and candidates' attempts to persuade voters through repetition of themes were less likely to be successful. The quandary is that journalistic standards, which bias the reporter in favor of writing about recent events and changes in positions, run counter to the needs of voters (as well as candidates) for readily available summaries of the candidates' positions when they are ready to make up their minds.

The problem is not easy for the press to deal with. The propensity of reporters is to seek out conflict and change, not the substance of issue positions already announced. Ostroff reported, on the basis of his study of local television coverage of a campaign, that:

The news persons believed that while they had a responsibility to inform their viewers about the campaigns, most of the candidates' activities were designed to achieve campaign goals, rather than to enlighten the public. One reporter who regularly covered the gubernatorial campaign sometimes expressed distaste at being assigned to some events; she said if the candidates wanted to "advertise" themselves, "let them buy the time."[13]

The media is as much concerned with the progress of the campaign as it is with its substance.

One cannot say that the press releases and the use of them by the news media were very helpful to voters in New Jersey in 1973. Information about issues in the releases was scarce to begin with, and the papers did not publish much discussion of the issues from the releases. Voters concerned with the future actions by either candidate, were he to have been elected, got little relevant information through this channel of communication. Voters did get a great deal of information designed to evoke a favorable reaction to the candidates' positions on the issues, but it did not help them make instrumental voting choices. Since the releases were basically propaganda, voters either thought they were receiving impartial information (in which case the weight they gave it was inconsistent with the weight they would have given it had they known its true nature), or they recognized the candidates' propaganda as such (in which case they could not tell which information was reliable).

But from the candidates' perspective, the releases were successful, especially if the measure of success is the amount of exposure they received through their releases. The exposure generated was substantial, and it reached voters when they were looking for news. The result is that candidates probably reach many of those whom they set out to contact with news releases. It is likely that few voters at all interested in campaigns in their areas did not read at least one news story based on a candidate press release.

To specify what the advantages of news releases are for campaigners, first, press releases allow candidates to offer interpretations of developments the press might cover anyway. If a prominent member of the opposition endorses a candidate, the press will report it, whether or not there is a release, but if the candidate provides a release, he can stress the reasons for the endorsement he would like to see emphasized and make appropriate quotations available for the press to use. By influencing the way in which the press writes the news, the voters may receive a picture of the development more favorable to the candidate than it might otherwise be.

Second, press releases can stimulate news coverage when there otherwise would be no story. The obvious situation where press releases are successful in this way is when a release is issued about a marginally newsworthy development. It is likely that few papers would have reporters covering it, but some papers may be glad to run a story about the event, using the release as its source, to provide its readers with wider coverage of the campaign. Releases may also stimulate coverage by providing an impetus to reporters. If a release is issued, some papers may pick it up, which makes it news; in that case, other reporters will want to write about the event too. In addition, weeklies may use releases merely because there is space to fill.

Third, sending releases of good quality regularly gives reporters and editors the impression that a well-run, efficient campaign is being conducted. Since one has a tendency to judge a complex phenomenon by one's response to the segments of it that one is familiar with, the press judges the campaign as a whole on the basis of its press operation.[14] The reporter's impression unavoidably colors his perception of the rest of the campaign. The support of the press is valuable, not merely because of endorsements or because of the added coverage the campaign may receive,[15] but because of the contagious optimism of newspaper reporters, an optimism often reflected in their news stories. Issuing releases is an important part of the campaign to win the support of the press.[16]

Fourth, campaign press releases are good vehicles for communicating to voters the notion that the candidate is running a viable campaign and that he has a good chance to win the election. Such an impression is helpful in motivating workers and in reinforcing voters faced with doubts about the wisdom of supporting a candidate whom his friends and associates may not support. The rationale is similar to the one justifying the use of such devices as bumper stickers—one must give the impression that the campaign is going well.[17] But the converse may be even a stronger reason to send a steady stream of good releases to the press: A candidate cannot afford to give the impression that his campaign is not going well. Such impressions are too easily created. Candidates must, therefore, keep their names in the news, and the specific content is not crucial for this purpose. Press releases serve the purpose well.

Finally, releases are an efficient tool to use what has been and remains an important source of information about campaigns for voters: their local newspaper. Of the various means available to candidates to stimulate news coverage, such as public appearances, press conferences, and granting interviews, among others, campaign releases have several advantages. They can reach more papers directly than any of the other methods, since they can be mailed to papers that cannot gather campaign news directly. They are inexpensive to produce and distribute, making them an excellent investment of campaign resources. In addition, only relatively important developments warrant calling news conferences, but even minor matters can be announced via press releases. As noted earlier, candidate news releases also give the campaigner greater influence over the final content of the news story generated.

Some suggestions for improving candidates' use of releases may be appropriate. These suggestions have one assumption in common.

Candidates will do better when releases are prepared and presented so that reporters and editors, judging them from the perspective of their requirements and standards, find them not only acceptable but attractive. To the extent that candidates can do so, while still including material designed to sway voters to their side, releases will deliver greater returns.

An obvious area where improvement is possible is in the way the releases are written; they should be written in good journalistic style. From the responses of editors to the surveys, it is clear that too many releases they receive are poorly written. If a poorly written release is not rejected immediately, it certainly needs to be rewritten, and the chance that the candidate's propaganda will survive is diminished. Furthermore, a well-written release reporting a minor event may be used, but a poorly written one requires an editor's time. Even if the event is more newsworthy, the release may not be used if the time to rewrite it is not available. Submitting a poorly prepared release in essence invites editorial rewriting and hands the control over the content to the newsperson. Good journalistic style calls for a lead paragraph that summarizes the essential facts and an inverted pyramid style, so that editors can cut the release "from the bottom" to fit available space without losing essential content. Writers should take the hint: The lower in the release a statement is, the less important the editor will think it is.

Campaign releases can also do better in meeting the press's need for hard news. The problem for candidates is that they want to spread the word about their qualifications for office, whether or not that is news, and voters who may want to have that information to help them choose between candidates need those facts whether or not they are news. Unfortunately, journalists react differently. The trick for candidates is to take advantage of journalists' idiosyncracies about what constitutes news.

There are two useful ways of doing so. One is to take advantage of newsworthy events that occur outside the campaign. Is that a local controversy that will allow the candidate to get involved long enough to announce his position on issues such as the one in dispute? Is there an unexpected development in politics or government, such as a controversial court decision or a scandal involving a high government official? The responses of candidates to such occurrences are newsworthy, and candidates should seize the opportunity to issue a statement. At the same time, they should insert relevant propaganda. Note, for instance, the way in which the Byrne release responded to the New Jersey Supreme Court decision in *Robinson* v. *Cahill*.[18] Even a well-known position is newsworthy under these circumstances, and candidates should not let such a chance go by.

Another way to take advantage of the journalists' own standards is to target releases: aim them at a specific audience the press also serves. Local groups, local events, and local residents should be emphasized whenever possible. A release announcing the formation of a statewide committee for some special interest group might be used by several major papers, but the same release that also mentions six or so committee members by name may be used by the same papers as well as by the home-town papers of each of the persons mentioned. Issuing a release in conjunction with the candidate's visit to a specific area, perhaps spotlighting a local person, is also an effective targeting technique. Excessive targeting may backfire; other papers may not pick up the release. If that is a possibility, the candidate can make a virtue out of necessity and simply head the release "Special to the Locality, Anystate, *Hometown Paper*." The local paper may feel sufficiently honored to use the release verbatim. Recent technological advances used to such advantage by direct mail specialists may also work well to help campaigners tailor releases to the newspaper it is sent to.

A further way to improve releases is to pay attention to deadlines. For instance, the deadlines for morning and evening papers are different, and candidates should take this difference into account. A release that is news in the afternoon may no longer be news the next morning. That means the afternoon and evening papers may use it, but it would probably not appear in the morning papers. Similarly, editors of weeklies dislike receiving releases that the dailies serving the same area have already used. Specifically, weeklies find it awkward to use releases that owe their news value to a specific event that may have already passed by the time the weekly can use the release. Writers, therefore, should avoid phrases that can date the release. To say that the candidate will, for instance, visit the state prison "Thursday" means that the release will become irrelevant after that day. Dailies can use it, but weeklies would prefer one that describes the response of the candidate to his visit— that release they can use even a week later.

The press can play a useful role in a democratic society by disseminating campaign information to voters. To the extent that it verifies the facts in a campaign communication before printing a story, that it reports fully what candidates have to say, that it is impartial between candidates, allowing the voter to choose, and that it provides relevant background information, the press can make an important contribution to the quality of political communication. The New Jersey press did well in these regards in 1973. It was because of its able performance of its task in dealing with the Sandman and Byrne releases that these releases were as useful as guides to the voters as they were. That they did not provide all of the information voters needed was not the fault of the press.

One should not expect voters to make instrumental voting decisions on the basis of the news stories stimulated by candidate news releases. Such stories and releases provide only part of the information voters require. Releases stress images (and report candidate qualifications) but not issues; news stories emphasize new developments and changes in positions, not consistency and continuity. The fault is not with the press releases alone; they are just not an efficient enough vehicle for communicating significant news. For stressing images and for keeping a candidate's name in the news, they work well, but for controversial statements, they give the press too much leeway, too much control over the final message. The press, on the other hand, is caught in its own dilemma. Either it provides current information about recent developments, competing with other news media to do so, or it provides the political information citizens need, whether it is news in the strict sense or not. Despite occasional attempts through round-up columns and so forth, the press has not reconciled these two functions. The result is that campaign releases facilitate only limited candidate appeals to voters and that voters who want to decide between candidates on substantive grounds must find the necessary information elsewhere.

Other methods of communicating in campaigns suffer from similar deficiencies. Campaign pamphlets, for instance, are probably more one-sided and filled with propaganda than are press releases, no doubt because of the lack of an intermediary to enforce standards of impartiality and accuracy. The difficulty arises out of the dual purpose of campaigns—not only do they serve to make information available to voters to enable them to choose, but they provide candidates with the opportunity to advance their personal goals and to do so by disseminating incomplete, inaccurate, or misleading information designed to increase their chances of winning the election.

But let's not end on a negative note. Campaign releases generate tremendous numbers of potential exposures, they reinforce themes developed in other areas of the campaign, and they aid candidates in building their images and increasing their name recognition. Releases do so well and they do so cheaply. Editors use them, and voters read the resulting stories. That makes it worth the effort for candidates, and that makes them worth studying by students of journalism, campaigning, and politics.

Based as these results are on a limited number of campaigns, we must be wary of generalizing too broadly. This study is more a foundation than a capstone. The use of candidate news releases as an example of communicating biased information through a neutral intermediary shares significant features with other means of communicating. Considered from one angle, the entire campaign is a media event, and the use of campaign releases is a small-scale example of it. The conclusions here, then, should be considered hypotheses about the campaigning process to be tested in future studies. If that happens, the foundation laid here may soon support a framework that will allow scholars to speak more forcefully, rather than tentatively, about the role of news releases in campaigning and about campaigning in general.

Appendix A

SURVEYING NEWSPAPER EDITORS

The evidence in chapter 5 comes from three separate surveys of newspaper editors. The first survey, conducted in late July and early August 1975, was sent to editors in New Jersey. The second survey, sent in June 1976, polled editors in Nebraska. The third survey, conducted in June 1980, was sent to a sample of editors nationwide. The reasons for conducting more than one survey was, first, to overcome some difficulties with the response rate in the New Jersey survey, particularly among daily editors; second, to be able to generalize more broadly; and third, to obtain more specific responses about the considerations involved in decisions about using candidate news releases. Categories were provided in closed-end questions in the later surveys, based on the comments editors made in response to open-end questions on earlier surveys. In this sense, the earlier surveys were a pretest for the national questionnaire.

The group of papers from which I drew my sample for the New Jersey questionnaire consisted of all of those that had referred to any of the candidates or their activities in the 1973 New Jersey gubernatorial campaign, a total of 276 weekly and daily papers. Since there were only 27 dailies, I sent a questionnaire to all of them. Approximately one-third of the 249 weekly editors received a questionnaire. The weeklies were divided into nine categories, by circulation and by estimated number of campaign releases they used. Circulation categories were under five thousand, over five thousand but under ten thousand, and over ten thousand. Release-use categories were none, one to three, and four or more.

Nebraska editors were not sampled. A questionnaire was sent to editors of all eighteen Nebraska daily papers and to all 185 editors of Nebraska weekly papers; editors who served more than one paper received only one questionnaire.

Using *Ayer's Directory of Publications* to draw the national sample, two hundred daily and two hundred weekly papers were randomly selected, excluding New Jersey and Nebraska editors, since they had been questioned before. Editors of dailies ranging in circulation from above six hundred thousand to three thousand and editors of weeklies ranging in circulation from above two hundred thousand to below one thousand received questionnaires.

Out of the 109 questionnaires sent to New Jersey editors, 48 were returned, for a response rate of 44.0 percent. The rate at which editors of weekly newspapers returned the questionnaire was markedly higher than the rate at which editors of dailies responded, although the difference was not statistically significant: $X^2_y = 2.3$, with 1 df. Only eight daily editors replied, for a return rate of 29.6 percent, but forty weekly editors sent a completed questionnaire back, for a return rate of 48.8 percent. For both editors of weekly papers and editors of daily papers, circulation or release use was unrelated to the return of the questionnaire.

All 18 daily editors returned a completed questionnaire in the Nebraska survey, and almost half (92 of 185) of the weekly editors did so. The return rate for weeklies in Nebraska differed markedly by circulation. Seventy percent of the largest third (circulation over two thousand) returned the questionnaire, but only 25 percent of the smallest third of the weeklies sent the survey back. Nebraska weeklies, however, are not nearly so large in circulation as New Jersey weeklies.

The return rate for the national survey was 42.25 percent; seventy-nine of the two hundred daily editors returned the survey, and ninety of the weekly editors responded, rates that are similar. Dividing each category into halves by circulation yields almost identical return rates. Thirty-nine of the editors of large dailies (circulation above fifteen thousand) returned questionnaires, as did forty of the small daily editors (circulation under fifteen thousand). Forty-six large weekly editors (circulation over thirty-five hundred) responded, and forty-four editors of small weekly papers (circulation under thirty-five hundred) did.

The response rate for the national survey is reassuring. Since in general the purpose is not to test hypotheses about editors' responses but to discover which factors editors consider relevant in dealing with releases and how they actually say they treat them, we may cautiously accept the conclusions the responses from these editors allow us to draw.

Appendix B

EXAMINING NEWSPAPER CLIPPINGS

The results on the use of the Byrne and Sandman releases are based on an examination of the clipping file collected by Representative Charles Sandman in his gubernatorial campaign. Sandman subscribed to a clipping service that sent him a copy of every mention it found in the press serving New Jersey (including relevant out-of-state papers) of either him or his opponent. I culled from this file those stories based on the releases.

There were a tremendous number of clippings. I did not count all of them, but I would estimate that approximately four thousand news stories were clipped and sent to Sandman. These clippings included news items from 314 publications, including several that seemed little more than mimeographed sheets.

The Bailey and Fithian results were based on access to the clippings their offices maintained. The Bailey clippings were thorough and voluminous, although not as numerous as the Sandman file. They were, however, not well identified. A sizable number of news stories based on the releases could not be identified by publication or date, although they could be classified by treatment of the release. The Fithian clippings were well organized, kept in file folders organized by topic.

The Inhofe results were based on clippings collected by Mike McCarvile from the major papers serving the First Oklahoma district. These clippings were not identified either by date or by paper. Only when the clipping itself included the date and name of the paper could I identify it. The Boren results were based on an examination of the clippings collected by the Oklahoma State Archives and kept with the documents from the Boren gubernatorial administration. These clippings proved difficult to use. Since Boren had only recently left office when I visited the archives, the staff had not had the opportunity to organize the Boren files as they would have liked.

Other results are based on a personal inspection of newspapers as available. Without clipping files based on a search of all papers serving a constituency, conclusions such as those reached in the Byrne, Sandman, and Bailey cases are virtually impossible. Unfortunately, few candidates maintain such files, and no one else has a reason to do so.

The accuracy of the results depends on the accuracy of the candidates' clipping services. The service Sandman used seemed to be thorough. In addition to the number of newspapers searched, one piece of evidence convinced me that more than a cursory service was provided. One clipping was included merely because several persons posed for a picture in front of a sign with Byrne's name on it—the picture itself was irrelevant to the gubernatorial campaign, but the service dutifully clipped and mailed it. Furthermore, the replies New Jersey editors gave when asked on the questionnaire whether they used Byrne or Sandman releases in 1973 were consistent with the pattern determined from the clippings, with only minor deviations.

The most important reason, however, for relying on the candidates' clipping services was one of efficiency. Personal visits to the morgues of even one state's dailies alone would have been prohibitive in time and money and would not have guaranteed that I would have been more alert to campaign news than the clipping service was. Since clipping services scan both the daily and weekly press, their product allowed me to speak of the coverage the Missouri press, for instance, gave the Bailey campaign, without having to generalize from too limited a selection of papers.

NOTES

CHAPTER 1

1. *The New York Times,* November 7, 1973, p. 1. For a report on the campaign, see Alvin Stephen Felzenberg, "The Impact of Gubernatorial Style on Policy Outcomes: An In Depth Study of Three New Jersey Governors" (Ph.D. diss., Princeton University, 1978), pp. 371-78.

2. John W. Kingdon, *Candidates for Office: Beliefs and Strategies* (New York: Random House, 1966), p. 109.

3. Nimmo defined a campaign as "the activities of an individual or group (the *campaigner*) in a particular context (the *campaign setting*) designed to manipulate the behavior of a wider number of people (the audience) to his advantage." Dan D. Nimmo, *The Political Persuaders: The Techniques of Modern Election Campaigns* (Englewood Cliffs, N.J.: Prentice-Hall, 1970), p. 10. I accept this definition with the proviso that campaign activities be described as coordinated. Cf. Robert Agranoff, *The Management of Election Campaigns* (Boston: Holbrook Press, 1976), p. 3: "A campaign is a coordinated effort to achieve some objective, such as electing a candidate to office.

4. Walter De Vries and Lance Tarrance, Jr., *The Ticket-Splitter: A New Face in American Politics* (Grand Rapids, Mich.: William B. Eerdmans Publishing Company, 1972), p. 73. Cf. Stanley Kelley, Jr., *Political Campaigning: Problems in Creating an Informed Electorate* (Washington, D.C.: The Brookings Institution, 1960), p. 8: "Campaign discussion should help voters make rational voting decisions. It has an informing function."

5. The basic argument on the impact of campaign consultants was made by Stanley Kelley, Jr., *Professional Public Relations and Political Power* (Baltimore: Johns Hopkins Press, 1956), ch. 7. See also David Lee Rosenbloom, *The Election Men: Professional Campaign Managers and American Democracy* (New York: Quadrangle Books, 1973). For advice on how to conduct a campaign using modern techniques, see, among others, Agranoff, *The Management of Election Campaigns;* Daniel M. Gaby and Merle H. Treusch, *Election Campaign Handbook* (Englewood Cliffs, N.J.: Prentice-Hall, 1976); Ray E. Hiebert et al., eds., *The Political Image*

Merchants: Strategies for the Seventies (Washington, D.C.: Acropolis Books, 1975); Edward Schwartzman, *Campaign Craftsmanship: A Professional's Guide to Campaigning for Elective Office* (New York: Universe Books, 1973); Arnold Steinberg, *The Political Campaign Handbook: Media, Scheduling, and Advance* (Lexington, Mass.: Lexington Books, 1976).

Of course, campaigners want to communicate with a number of groups, and voters comprise only one. It is possible to speak of different campaigns aimed at each such group. Kelley distinguished five such campaigns. Cf. Stanley Kelley, Jr., "Campaign Propaganda in Perspective," in *The President: Rex, Princeps, Imperator?* ed. Joseph M. Ray (El Paso, Tex.: Texas Western Press, 1969), pp. 59-67.

6. McGuire and Papegeorgis reported that subjects are less likely to change their attitudes if they are forewarned that their beliefs would be attacked. William J. McGuire and Demetrios Papegeorgis, "Effectiveness of Forewarning in Developing Resistance to Persuasion," *Public Opinion Quarterly* 26 (1962): 24-34.

7. Charles W. Smith, Jr., "Campaign Communication Media," *The Annals of the American Academy of Political and Social Science* 259 (1948): 91.

8. De Vries and Tarrance, *The Ticket-Splitter,* p. 78. See their chart on page 77.

9. Ibid. Patterson and McClure drew a different conclusion from their study of the impact of television newscasts and television campaign advertisements. They found campaign spots to be a better source of information for voters than network news broadcasts. Thomas E. Patterson and Robert D. McClure, *The Unseeing Eye: The Myth of Television Power in National Politics* (New York: G. P. Putnam's Sons, 1976).

10. Gaby and Treusch, *Election Campaign Handbook,* p. 147.

11. Not to mention that the *format* of the message must be appropriate.

12. Some advertising media will refuse some advertisements, but campaigners generally have substantial leeway.

13. Timothy Crouse, *The Boys on the Bus* (New York: Ballantine Books, 1973), p. 150.

14. Conrad Joyner, *The American Politician* (Tucson, Ariz.: The University of Arizona Press, 1971), p. 178.

15. See Ralph D. Casey, "Party Campaign Propaganda," *The Annals of the American Academy of Political and Social Science* 179 (1935): 100-101: "From July 1 to November 2, 1928, the Democratic bureau issued between 1,000 and 1,500 news releases. . . . By October 10, 1928, the Washington Bureau of the Republican Committee had issued 1,300 news and feature releases."

16. Interview with Harold V. Hunter, June 25, 1980.

17. Gaby and Treusch, *Election Campaign Handbook,* p. 147.

18. Deckelnick suggested several advantages of releases in organizing the facts for reporters. For instance, he suggested that if news calls for a quotation from the opponent, the release provide it so that it can emphasize it according to the campaigner's criteria. "What's the difference? If it's an important story—page one— maybe [the opponent's] remarks are low in the story, not on page one but where the story is continued, where not everyone will read them." Gary Deckelnick, "The Candidate and the Media," *Campaign Insight* 9, no. 16 (August 15, 1978): 10.

19. See, among others, Agranoff, *The Management of Election Campaigns*; Chester G. Atkins, with Barry Hock and Bob Martin, *Getting Elected: A Guide to Winning State and Local Office* (Boston: Houghton Mifflin Company, 1973);

James Brown and Philip M. Seib, *The Art of Politics: Electoral Strategies and Campaign Management* (Port Washington, N.Y.: Alfred Publishing Company, 1976); Democratic State Committee of New Jersey, *Election Workshop Manual: The Communications Handbook* (Trenton, N.J., no date); Frederik Pohl, *Practical Politics 1972: How to Make Politics and Politicians Work for You* (New York: Ballantine Books, 1971); Steinberg, *Political Campaign Handbook*.

20. Lynda Lee Kaid, "Newspaper Treatment of a Candidate's News Releases," *Journalism Quarterly* 53 (1976): 135-37. John H. Bolen, "Daily Newspaper Coverage of the 1970 Texas Gubernatorial Campaign" (M.A. thesis, University of Texas, 1970), p. 87.

21. Interview with Harold V. Hunter, June 25, 1980.

22. I shall discuss the concept of "hard news" in chapters 2 and 5.

23. On "gatekeepers" in the press, see David Manning White, "The 'Gatekeeper': A Case Study in the Selection of News," *Journalism Quarterly* 27 (1950): 283-90.

24. Casey, "Party Campaign Propaganda," p. 100.

25. Lasswell is cited in L. John Martin, "Recent Theory on Mass Media Potential in Political Campaigns," *The Annals of the American Academy of Political and Social Science* 427 (1976): 126.

26. See the recent book on the media and the White House in this context: Michael Baruch Grossman and Martha Joynt Kumar, *Portraying the President: The White House and the News Media* (Baltimore: Johns Hopkins University Press, 1981).

27. See chapter 2 for a discussion of journalistic standards.

28. Among those who discuss the benefits of incumbency, see Robert J. Huckshorn and Robert C. Spencer, *The Politics of Defeat: Campaigning for Congress* (Amherst, Mass.: University of Massachusetts Press, 1971), p. 91; David A. Leuthold, *Electioneering in a Democracy: Campaigns for Congress* (New York: John Wiley & Sons, 1968), pp. 122-23; and Nelson W. Polsby and Aaron Wildavsky, *Presidential Elections: Strategies of American Electoral Politics,* 4th ed. (New York: Charles Scribner's Sons, 1976), pp. 72-74.

29. Interview with Reginald Todd, June 19, 1980.

30. Frost reported that 90 percent of county party leaders rate newspaper publicity "really useful" in New Jersey. Cf. Richard T. Frost, "Stability and Change in Local Party Politics," *Public Opinion Quarterly* 25 (1961): 221-35.

31. Peter Clarke and Eric Fredin, "Newspapers, Television and Political Reasoning," *Public Opinion Quarterly* 42 (1978): 145.

32. Richard F. Hixson, "A Brief Look at New Jersey's Prosperous Daily Press," *Journalism Quarterly* 43 (1966): 765-69.

CHAPTER 2

1. Walter Lippmann, *Public Opinion* (New York: Harcourt, Brace and Company, 1922), p. 320. Cf. also Anthony Downs, *An Economic Theory of Democracy* (New York: Harper & Row, 1957), pt. 3, on the costs of being informed.

2. I use the term *press* here to refer to periodicals that purport to report the news to their readers. We must remember, too, that candidates and officials both publish leaflets and pamphlets to communicate with the public.

3. Thomas Schroth, "The Role of the Press in a Democratic Government,"

in *The Press in Washington,* ed. Eldon Hiebart (New York: Dodd, Mead and Company, 1966), p. 2.

4. James B. Reston, "The Job of the Reporter," in the Staff of the *New York Times, The Newspaper: Its Making and Its Meaning* (New York: Charles Scribner's Sons, 1955), pp. 92-93.

5. Fred S. Siebert, "The Libertarian Theory of the Press," in *Four Theories of the Press,* by Fred S. Siebert et al. (Urbana, Ill.: University of Illinois Press, 1956), pp. 39-71.

6. Ibid., p. 56.

7. George Anastaplo, "Self-Government and the Mass Media: A Practical Man's Guide," in *The Mass Media and Modern Democracy,* ed. Harry M. Clor (Chicago: Rand McNally, 1974), p. 163. See also Reston, "The Job of the Reporter," p. 93: "The first article of the Bill of Rights was placed there as a pledge of safety to the *people,* and . . . therefore the primary obligation of the newspaper in general and of the reporter in particular is *to the people."*

8. *New York Times Company* v. *Sullivan,* 376 U.S. 254 (1964), at 269. For arguments in favor of a free press where there is no constitutional guarantee, see the opinions of Canadian Chief Justice Lyman Poore Duff and Associate Justice Lawrence A. D. Cannon in *Reference re Alberta Statutes* [1938] S.C.R. 100.

9. Lippmann, *Public Opinion,* p. 354. Cohen noted that the press has a policy impact by its choices on what to print: "As long as the press can endow an event with political significance by the process of giving it wide currency, this question of the character of press coverage of foreign policy is a serious one." Bernard C. Cohen, "The Press and Foreign Policy in the United States," in *Foreign Policy in American Government,* ed. Bernard C. Cohen (Boston: Little, Brown and Company, 1965), p. 201. Lippman's comments suggest the agenda-setting function for the press.

10. Paul H. Weaver, "The Politics of a News Story," in Clor, *The Mass Media,* p. 88.

11. See, for instance, Maxwell E. McCombs and Donald R. Shaw, "The Agenda-Setting Function of Mass Media," *Public Opinion Quarterly* 36 (1972): 176-87.

12. On the concept of the "gatekeeper," see David Manning White, "The 'Gate-Keeper': A Case Study in the Selection of News," *Journalism Quarterly* 27 (1950): 283-90; Abraham Z. Bass, "Refining the 'Gate-Keeper' Concept: a UN Radio Case Study," *Journalism Quarterly* 46 (1969): 69-74; Morris Janowitz, "Professional Models in Journalism: The Gatekeeper and the Advocate," *Journalism Quarterly* 52 (1975): 618-26, 662.

13. Bernard C. Cohen, *The Press and Foreign Policy* (Princeton, N.J.: Princeton University Press, 1963), p. 54. This book deserves its reputation as one of the best treatments of the press ever written.

14. Warren Breed, "Analyzing News: Some Questions for Research," *Journalism Quarterly* 33 (1956): 447.

15. Cohen, *The Press and Foreign Policy,* p. 59.

16. See, among others, Breed, "Analyzing News," p. 477; Anju Chaudhary, "Comparative News Judgment of Indian and American Journalists," *Gazette* 20 (1974): 240n; Susan H. Miller, "News Coverage of Congress: The Search for the Ultimate Spokesman," *Journalism Quarterly* 54 (1977): 459; Cohen, *The Press and Foreign Policy,* pp. 55-57; and Doris A. Graber, *Mass Media and American Politics* (Washington, D.C.: CQ Press, 1980), pp. 62-68.

Another explanation for similarity of news judgments is pack journalism. For a treatment, see Timothy Crouse, *The Boys on the Bus* (Ballantine Books, 1973), pp. 7-15 and passim.

17. Ibid., p. 19.

18. Delmer D. Dunn, *Public Officials and the Press* (Reading, Mass.: Addison-Wesley Publishing Company, 1969), p. 27.

19. E. E. Schattschneider, *The Semi-Sovereign People* (Hindsdale, Ill.: Dryden Press, 1975), p. 1.

20. Downs, *An Economic Theory,* ch. 3, argued, however, that only the issues on which the candidates or parties differ are important to voters.

21. Walter Gieber, "Across the Desk: A Study of 16 Telegraph Editors," *Journalism Quarterly* 33 (1956): 423-32, commented on p. 430: "The pertinent value was 'consequence'—the factor of importance to the largest number of persons."

22. Dunn, *Public Officials,* p. 25. Emphasis added.

23. Cohen, *The Press and Foreign Policy,* p. 55.

24. Dunn, *Public Officials,* pp. 25-26.

25. Herbert J. Gans, *Deciding What's News: A Study of CBS Evening News, NBC Nightly News, Newsweek, and Time* (New York: Pantheon Books, 1979), p. 9.

26. Lippmann, *Public Opinion,* p. 358.

27. For a treatment of the McCarthy phenomenon, see Richard H. Rovere, *Senator Joe McCarthy* (New York: World Publishing Company, 1959).

28. Ibid., p. 165.

29. Crouse, *The Boys on the Bus,* p. 323.

30. Richard Bolling, *House Out of Order* (New York: E. P. Dutton & Company, 1966), p. 145.

31. Joel Swerdlow, "The Decline of the Boys on the Bus," *Washington Journalism Review* 3, no. 1 (1981): 18.

32. Lucian W. Pye, "The Emergence of Professional Communicators," in *Communication and Political Development,* ed. Lucian W. Pye (Princeton, N.J.: Princeton University Press, 1963), p. 78.

33. Bernard Roshco, *Newsmaking* (Chicago: University of Chicago Press, 1975), p. 53. Original in italics; ch. 4 discusses objective news reporting. See also James David Barber, "Characters in the Campaign: The Literary Problem," in *Race for the Presidency: The Media and the Nominating Process,* ed. James David Barber (Englewood Cliffs, N.J.: Prentice-Hall, 1978), pp. 111-46.

34. Roshco, *Newsmaking,* p. 41.

35. Dan D. Nimmo, *Newsgathering in Washington: A Study in Political Communication* (New York: Atherton Press, 1964), pp. 32-33.

36. Ben H. Bagdikian, "The Fruits of Agnewism," *Columbia Journalism Review* 11 (1973): 10.

37. Paul H. Weaver, "The New Journalism and the Old," in *Ethics and the Press: Readings in Mass Media Morality,* ed. John C. Merrill and Ralph D. Barney (New York: Hastings House Publishers, 1975), p. 95.

38. Dunn, *Public Officials,* p. 22.

39. Siebert, "The Libertarian Theory," p. 51.

40. William L. Rivers, *The Adversaries: Politics and the Press* (Boston: Beacon Press, 1970).

41. Dunn, *Public Officials,* p. 80.

42. Elmer E. Cornwell, Jr., "Role of the Press in Presidential Politics," in *Politics and the Press,* ed. Richard W. Lee (Washington, D.C.: Acropolis Books, 1970), p. 18.

43. Michael Baruch Grossman and Martha Joynt Kumar, *Portraying the President: The White House and the News Media* (Baltimore: Johns Hopkins University Press, 1981), p. 13.

44. Nimmo, *Newsgathering,* pp. 6-7.

45. Dunn, *Public Officials,* p. 11.

46. Rivers, *The Adversaries,* p. 47.

47. Grossman and Kumar, *Portraying the President,* p. 5.

48. Jules Witcover, *Marathon: The Pursuit of the Presidency, 1972-1976* (New York: The Viking Press, 1977), p. 557.

49. Gans, *Deciding What's News,* p. 291.

50. Ibid.

51. Joseph Pulitzer, "Accuracy, Accuracy, Accuracy," in *Newsmen Speak: Journalists on Their Craft,* ed. Edmond D. Coblentz (Berkeley, Calif.: University of California Press, 1954), p. 12.

52. Loren Ghiglinoe, ed., *Evaluating the Press: The New England Daily Newspaper Survey* (Southbridge, Mass.: New England Daily Newspaper Survey, 1973), p. 5.

CHAPTER 3

1. Brendan Byrne News Release, 1 October 1973, "Byrne Calls for Quick Action." (Byrne releases will hereafter be cited BR, the date, and a key word title. Sandman releases will be cited SR and the corresponding information.) On the new New York drug statutes, see also "Governor Signs His Drug Bills and Assails the Critics Again," *New York Times,* May 9, 1973, p. 1.

2. BR, 2 October 1973, "Del Deo Appointed."

3. BR, 2 October 1973, "Communication Workers."

4. SR, 1 October 1973, "Sandman Warns."

5. SR, 3 October 1973, "Arthur Miller Named"; SR, 5 October 1973, "Byrne Is Ducking."

6. See note 3, chapter 1.

7. Interview with Herb Wolfe, July 10, 1975. The release in question was BR, 14 August 1973, "Amusement Rides."

8. For a discussion on the use of significance tests for this purpose, see Edward R. Tufte, "Improving Data Analysis in Political Science," *World Politics* 21 (1969): 641-54.

9. Copies of these releases were made available to me through the kindness of Kathy Forsyth of the Byrne campaign and J. Fred Coldren of the Sandman campaign.

10. Sandman also issued seventy-four Notices of Appearance, but Byrne did not issue any. These notices are not examined further in this study.

11. Kathleen Crow made the Antonovich releases available, Mike McCarvile the Inhofe releases, Jonathan C. Levin the Specter releases, and Duane Benton the Bailey releases. I was placed on the mailing list for the Anderson releases through the good offices of Clifford Brown.

12. Interview with Max Besler, November 24, 1980.

13. Comments by district office employee, November 24, 1980.

14. Interview with Judy Johnson, November 25, 1980.

15. Personal communication, Mark Elam, aide to Ron Paul, November 25, 1980.

16. Telephone interview with Reginald Todd, district aide to J. J. Pickle, June 19, 1980.

17. James Brown and Philip M. Seib, *The Art of Politics: Electoral Strategies and Campaign Management* (Port Washington, N.Y.: Alfred Publishing Company, 1976), p. 117. See the results presented in chapter 5.

18. Michael Baruch Grossman and Martha Joynt Kumar, *Portraying the Presidency: The White House and the News Media* (Baltimore: Johns Hopkins University Press, 1981), p. 30.

19. Two Byrne releases and one Sandman release neither included a date nor could be classified by date on the basis of other information.

20. Telephone interview with Ernie Stromberger, June 23, 1980.

21. Interviews with Kathy Forsyth, August 16, 1977, and Richard Leone, August 19, 1977.

22. Interview with J. Fred Coldren, August 17, 1977.

23. "G.O.P. Leaders Say Sandman Is Facing a Major Defeat," *New York Times,* October 28, 1973, p. 1.

24. Arnold Steinberg, *The Political Campaign Handbook: Media, Scheduling, and Advance* (Lexington, Mass.: Lexington Books, 1976), p. 48.

25. BR, 7 October 1973, "Byrne Calls Sandman's Tax Increase Plan."

26. BR, 22 October 1973, "CWA Locals."

27. SR, 29 October 1973, "Diverted from Tax Issue."

28. SR, 18 October 1973, "Nursing Homes." Of course, there is an important message implicit in this release: Sandman cares enough about the residents of nursing homes to appoint someone to help them file absentee ballots.

CHAPTER 4

1. Leo C. Rosten, *The Washington Correspondents* (New York: Arno Press, 1974), p. 73.

2. David L. Paletz, "Candidates and the Media in the 1976 Presidential Election," *Parties and Elections in an Anti-Party Age: American Politics and the Crisis of Confidence,* ed. Jeff Fishel (Bloomington, Ind.: Indiana University Press, 1978), p. 259.

3. Roy E. Carter, Jr., "Newspaper 'Gatekeepers' and the Sources of News," *Public Opinion Quarterly* 22 (1958): 133-44.

4. See Ole R. Holsti, *Content Analysis for the Social Sciences and Humanities* (Reading, Mass.: Addison-Wesley Publishing Company, 1969).

5. BR, 10 September 1973, "Salem County Republican."

6. BR, 26 July 1973, "Leslie Blau."

7. BR, 10 September 1973, "UAW."

8. BR, 2 October 1973, "Communications Workers."

9. BR, 22 October 1973, "United Transportation Union."

10. BR, 22 October 1973, "CWA Locals."

11. BR, 30 September 1973, "Carpenters Education Committee."

12. BR, 14 August 1973, "Mayor of Princeton."

13. SR, 26 October 1973, "PBA Illegal Endorsement."

14. SR, 25 October 1973, "Experience an Issue."

15. SR, 18 September 1973, "Fiscal Responsibility."

16. SR, 18 September 1973, "Rockefeller."

17. SR, 21 September 1973, "Boss Controlled."

18. See p. 62.

19. SR, 17 October 1973, "Pledges to Stop Income Tax."

20. SR, 20 September 1973, "Opposes Income Tax."

21. SR, 12 October 1973, "Save Harmless."

22. SR, 25 October 1973, "N.J. Citizens."

23. Mike Antonovich release (hereafter cited as MAR), 18 September 1980, "Hefty Turnout."

24. MAR, 25 September 1980, "Movable Evening Board Meetings."

25. Wendell Bailey release (hereafter cited as WBR), no date, "Chamber of Commerce"; WBR, no date, "Rolla Paper Endorses"; WBR, no date, "Township Endorses."

26. BR, 10 September 1973, "UAW."

27. BR, 26 July 1973, "Leslie Blau."

28. BR, 5 October 1973, "Conservative Morris Republican."

29. BR, 12 July 1973, "Ann Klein."

30. BR, 12 September 1973, "Former Case Campaign Director"; BR, 8 October 1973, "Sandman Misleads"; BR, 25 September 1973, "Chatham Republican."

31. BR, 21 August 1973, "Mercer Republican."

32. SR, 3 October 1973, "Councilman Maresca."

33. SR, 25 October 1973, "Experience an Issue."

34. SR, 20 September 1973, "Opposes Income Tax."

35. SR, 23 August 1973, "United Afro American Association."

36. SR, 18 October 1973, "Byrne 'Flipper.' "

37. SR, 25 October 1973, "N.J. Citizens."

38. SR, 27 September 1973, "Prominent Democrats."

39. SR, 27 September 1973, "Prominent Democrats."

40. SR, 25 October 1973, "N.J. Citizens."

41. MAR, 14 March 1980, "Poll Shows"; MAR, 29 April 1980, "Work-for-Welfare."

42. BR, 14 June 1973, "Byrne Calls for 'New Beginning.' "

43. BR, 27 September 1973, "Housing Strategy"; BR, 16 October 1973, "Homeowners Bill of Rights."

44. SR, 24 October 1973, "Sandman Defends Home Rule."

45. SR, 28 June 1973, "Sandman Blasts Demo Hint."

46. SR, 25 October 1973, "Sandman Pledges End."

47. SR, 24 October 1973, "Sandman Defends Home Rule."

48. SR, 12 October 1973, "Sandman Promises Assistance."

49. BR, 24 September 1973, "Phillipsburg Education Association." Emphasis added.

50. BR, 15 September 1973, "Former Cahill Aide,"; BR, 17 September 1973, "Sussex Republican."

51. BR, 26 July 1973, "Leslie Blau."

52. BR, 19 June 1973, *"Robinson v. Cahill."*

53. BR, 23 August 1973, "Budget Surplus."

54. BR, 14 June 1973, "Byrne Calls for 'New Beginning.' "

55. BR, 19 June 1973, *"Robinson v. Cahill."*

56. SR, 1 November 1973, "Referendum on Income Tax."

57. SR, 18 September 1973, "Fiscal Responsibility."

58. SR, 4 November 1973, "Sandman Pledges 'No Income Tax.' "

59. SR, 25 October 1973, "Sandman Pledges End."

60. Quoted in SR, 28 June 1973, "Sandman Blasts Demo Hint."

61. Ibid.

62. SR, 1 November 1973, "Referendum on Income Tax."

63. SR, 1 October 1973, "Byrne Would Increase Property Taxes."

64. Quoted in BR, 5 October 1973, "Sandman's Plan 'Incredible.' "

65. Ibid.

66. BR, 30 July 1973, "PATH Fare Hike."

67. SR, 30 July 1973, "PATH Fare Hike."

68. Ibid.

69. BR, 7 August 1973, "Public Transportation Commitment."

70. BR, 24 September 1973, "Transportation Program."

71. Ibid.

72. Ibid.

73. SR, 29 September 1973, "Sandman Wants Rail Merger."

74. Ibid.

75. SR, 29 October 1973, "Port Authority Commissioner."

76. Ibid.

77. Pat Roberts release (hereafter cited as PRR), 30 June 1980, "Water."

78. John Anderson release (hereafter cited as AR), 8 October 1980, "New Right"; AR, 17 October 1980, "Persian Gulf."

79. Mike Andrews release (hereafter cited as AWR), 9 October 1980, "Oil Spills."

80. AWR, 18 October 1980, "Harris County Blacks."

81. Arlen Specter release (hereafter cited as ASR), 19 August 1980, "Apparel Industry,"; ASR, 30 July 1980, "Buy American Legislation,"; ASR, 3 April 1980, "Mushroom Industry."

82. LeRoy C. Ferguson and Ralph H. Smuckler, *Politics in the Press: An Analysis of Press Content in 1952 Senatorial Campaigns* (East Lansing, Mich.: The Governmental Research Bureau, Michigan State College, 1954), p. 75.

83. MAR, 14 March 1980, "Poll Shows."

84. BR, 14 June 1973, "Byrne Calls for 'New Beginning.' "

85. For example, Ronald Reagan release (hereafter cited as RR), 5 May 1980, "Department of Education."

86. Joel Swerdlow, "The Decline of the Boys on the Bus," *Washington Journalism Review* 3, no. 1 (1981): 16.

87. Ibid., p. 17.

88. Jim Inhofe release (hereafter cited as IR), 13 September 1976, "ACU Endorsement,"; PRR, 6 October 1980, "VFW Endorsement."

89. Paul H. Weaver, "The Politics of a News Story, in *The Mass Media and Mod-*

ern Democracy, ed. Harry M. Clor (Chicago: Rand McNally, 1974), pp. 85-112.

90. John Hohenberg, *The Professional Journalist,* 2nd ed. (New York: Holt, Rinehart and Winston, 1969), p. 302.

91. Greg Carman release (hereafter cited as CR), 8 April 1980, "Mercadante Endorsement."

92. See the discussion of questionnaire responses in chapter 5.

93. Frederik Pohl, *Practical Politics 1972: How to Make Politics and Politicians Work for You* (New York: Ballantine Books, 1970), p. 176.

94. BR, 10 September 1973, "Byrne Picks Santos."

95. See chapter 6. See also the results by Lynda Lee Kaid, "Newspaper Treatment of a Candidate's News Releases," *Journalism Quarterly* 53 (1976): 135-37; and by John H. Bolen, "Daily Newspaper Coverage of the 1970 Texas Gubernatorial Campaign" (M.A. thesis, University of Texas, 1970).

CHAPTER 5

1. Releases and news stories in question are SR, 16 October 1973, "Handicapped Bond Referendum"; "Sandman in War on Pushers," Jersey City, N.J., *Jersey Journal,* October 16, 1973; "Endorses Handicapped Referendum," *Glen Ridge* (N.J.) *Paper,* October 18, 1973; BR, 21 August 1973, "Transit Union"; "Transit Local Backs Byrne," *Newark* (N.J.) *Star-Ledger,* August 21, 1973; "Byrne Endorsed by Union," Atlantic City, N.J., *Greater Atlantic City Reporter,* August 29, 1973.

2. Frank Allen, "News Releases from Business Irritate Editors," *Wall Street Journal,* May 20, 1981, p. 27.

3. Quotations otherwise unattributed in this chapter come from responses to the questionnaires; editors involved will remain anonymous.

4. David Manning White, "The 'Gate-Keeper': A Case Study in the Selection of News," *Journalism Quarterly* 27 (1950): 287.

5. Richard R. Nicolai and Sam G. Riley, "The Gatekeeping Function from the Point of View of the PR Man," *Journalism Quarterly* 49 (1972): 371-73.

6. Questionnaire response, New Jersey, 1975.

7. Arnold Steinberg, *The Political Campaign Handbook: Media, Scheduling, and Advance* (Lexington, Mass.: Lexington Books, 1976), p. 25.

8. Questionnaire response, New Jersey, 1975.

9. Interview with Harold V. Hunter, June 25, 1980.

10. Questionnaire response, Nebraska, 1976.

11. Ibid.

12. Ibid.

CHAPTER 6

1. F. Christopher Arterton, "Campaign Organizations Confront the Media-Political Environment," in *Race for the Presidency: The Media and the Nominating Process,* ed. James David Barber (Englewood Cliffs, N.J.: Prentice-Hall, 1978), pp. 3-25.

2. For instance, although Sandman subscribed to a clipping service so that he could keep track of how the press covered him, most of the envelopes the service mailed him were unopened the summer after the election.

3. Thanks to J. Fred Coldren for access to the Sandman clipping file, to Duane Benton for access to the Bailey materials, and to Susan Clark Etter for access to the Fithian clippings. See appendix B for a discussion of access to campaign news items.

4. Lynda Lee Kaid, "Newspaper Treatment of a Candidate's News Releases," *Journalism Quarterly* 53 (1976): 136.

5. Since one item could use material from more than one release, the total number of release uses is greater than the total number of news items.

6. See chapter 5, p. 76.

7. Coldren suggested that this consideration was relevant. Interview with J. Fred Coldren, August 17, 1977.

8. The correlations between the number of releases issued a week with the number of news items based on releases (but not necessarily that week's releases) appearing that week for Sandman was .897 and .454 for Byrne.

9. Such purposes exist; among others are taking advantage of a slow news day, reaching a particular group by announcing an appointment or an endorsement, or publicizing an upcoming event.

10. "Trying Very Hard," *Glen Ridge* (New Jersey) *Paper,* October 18, 1973.

11. Ibid.

12. BR, 11 October 1973, "Glick Named." A Sandman release could have been as easily chosen.

13. William P. Martin and Michael V. Singletary, "Newspaper Treatment of State Government Releases," *Journalism Quarterly* 58 (1981): 94.

14. BR, 11 October 1973, "Glick Named."

15. Deckelnick offered candidates this advice: "Once you have established that the newspaper prints everything verbatim, take advantage of that fact. Use adjectives, normally frowned on by newspapers. And do not attribute. Instead of writing, 'Smith said John Jones is an intelligent candidate,' write simply, 'John Jones is an intelligent candidate.' If the newspaper is silly enough to let that statement slip into print it will have more credibility. It will appear the assessment is that of the newspaper and not of a candidate's press aide." Gary Deckelnick, "Dealing with the Small Weekly Editor," *Campaign Insight* 9, no. 22 (November 15, 1978): 7.

16. RR, 14 May 1980, "Economy and Unemployment"; Richard Bergholz, "Reagan Eludes Specifics as He Meets Michigan Auto Workers," *Los Angeles Times,* May 15, 1980, pt. 1, p. 18.

17. RR, 2 May 1980, "Carter's Energy Plan"; William Endicott, "Reagan Rules Out Military Force in Iran," *Los Angeles Times,* May 3, 1980, pt. 1, p. 12.

18. Allen F. Yoder, "Green Street Overpass Pledged by Byrne." *Woodbridge* (New Jersey) *News Tribune,* October 4, 1973.

19. Stanley E. Laffin press release, undated, "Announces Candidacy"; "Laffin Seeks Senate Seat," *Westbrook* (Maine) *American Journal,* June 4, 1980, p. 19.

20. "Sandman Taps Kearny Mayor," *Bayonne* (New Jersey) *Facts,* August 29, 1973.

21. SR, 22 August 1973, "Cavalier."

22. See, for instance, the suggestion Steinberg made on writing releases so that they can be "cut from the bottom," which he called the inverted pyramid style: "each succeeding paragraph is less important than the one above it. The theory is that

an editor pressed by space considerations can cut the typewritten story from the end." Arnold Steinberg, *The Political Campaign Handbook: Media, Scheduling, and Advance* (Lexington, Mass.: Lexington Books, 1976), p. 75 (emphasis deleted).

23. SR, 28 August 1973, "Mrs. Bassett."

24. "Local Lady Aids Sandman's Bid," *Morristown* (New Jersey) *Daily Record,* August 30, 1973.

25. BR, 2 September 1973, "Essex Republican."

26. "GOP Leader Backs Byrne," *Montclair* (New Jersey) *Times,* September 6, 1973.

27. IR, 13 September 1976, "ACU Endorsement."

28. "Inhofe Gets Backing of Lobby Unit," *Tulsa Tribune,* September 13, 1976.

29. SR, 23 August 1973, "United Afro-American Association."

30. "Afro Americans Back Sandman," *Red Bank* (New Jersey) *Register,* August 28, 1973.

31. BR, 10 September 1973, "Di Nicola."

32. "Di Nicola Backs Brendan Byrne," Salem, New Jersey, *Today's Sunbeam,* September 14, 1973; BR, 10 September 1973, "Di Nicola."

33. BR, 22 July 1973, "Marciante."

34. "AFL-CIO Chief Blasts Sandman," Vineland, New Jersey, *Vineland Times Journal,* July 24, 1973; BR, 22 July 1973, "Marciante."

35. SR, 27 September 1973, "Prominent Democrats."

36. "Sandman Supporters Cite Far Left and Radical Chique," *Toms River* (New Jersey) *Reporter,* October 3, 1973.

37. BR, 23 August 1973, "Surplus."

38. "Byrne's Plan for Surplus," *Newark* (New Jersey) *Star-Ledger,* August 23, 1973.

39. "Don't Spend the Surplus, Sandman Urges Cahill," *The Hackensack* (New Jersey) *Record,* August 24, 1973.

40. SR, 25 October 1973, "Non-Resident Taxation."

41. Ibid.

42. "Sandman Pledges to End Out-of-State Taxation," *Camden* (New Jersey) *Courier-Post,* October 25, 1973.

43. SR, 20 September 1973, "Opposes Income Tax."

44. "Sandman Says Byrne Late on No Tax Stand," Trenton, New Jersey, *The Trentonian,* September 21, 1973.

45. SR, 1 November 1973, "Election Will Be Referendum."

46. "Sandman Says Election Tues. Is Referendum on Income Tax," *Lambertville,* New Jersey, *Beacon,* November 1, 1973.

47. SR, 1 November 1973, "Election Will Be Referendum."

48. BR, 24 September 1973, "A Transportation Program."

49. Ibid; "Rail Takeover Plan Unveiled by Byrne," *The Elizabeth* (New Jersey) *Daily Journal,* September 25, 1973; "Byrne Rail Plan Challenges PA," Trenton, New Jersey, *Trenton Evening Times,* September 25, 1973.

50. SR, 29 September 1973, "Rail Merger."

51. SR, 29 October 1973, "Port Authority Commissioner."

52. "Sandman Gets Hoffman's Support," *Red Bank* (New Jersey) *Register,* October 29, 1973; "Hoffman Backs Sandman," Jersey City, New Jersey, *The Jersey Journal,* October 29, 1973.

53. "Hoffman Backs Sandman.'

54. "Sandman Gets Hoffman's Support."

55. "Reagan, Anderson Prepare for Debate," *Kansas City Star,* September 18, 1980, p. 12A.

56. David Boren release (hereafter cited as DBR), 10 August 1978, "Charge by Points."

57. The stories appeared in the Tulsa *Tribune,* August 11, 1978, the *Oklahoma City Journal,* August 11, 1978, and the *Oklahoma City Times,* August 10, 1978.

58. DBR, 23 August 1978, "Affidavit."

59. The stories appeared in the *Tulsa Tribune,* August 21, 1978, the *Oklahoma City Daily Oklahoman,* August 24, 1978, and the *Oklahoma City Journal,* August 24, 1978.

CHAPTER 7

1. The source for the data was the endorsement editorials included in the Sandman clipping file. Twenty-nine editorials endorsing one candidate or another were included. The *Newark Star-Ledger* did not endorse a gubernatorial candidate in 1973.

2. See pp. 76-77.

3. Ann Gregory, editor, St. Paul, Virginia, *Clinch Valley Times,* comments to questionnaire.

4. I drew the line separating northern and southern New Jersey between Burlington and Ocean Counties on the south and Mercer and Monmouth Counties on the north. There are eight counties in the southern half and thirteen counties north of this line.

CHAPTER 8

1. On the notion of "rational" in this context, see Anthony Downs, *An Economic Theory of Democracy* (New York: Harper & Row, 1957), pp. 4-8.

2. Patterson and McClure argued that television commercials were better sources of information about candidates and issues than were network newscasts for voters in the 1972 Presidential election. See Thomas E. Patterson and Robert D. McClure, *The Unseeing Eye: The Myth of Television Power in National Elections* (New York: G. P. Putnam's Sons, 1976).

3. Baxter Ward, quoted in Douglas Shuit, "Antonovich Gets Reagan Endorsement," *Los Angeles Times,* May 13, 1980, pt. 1, p. 14.

4. One side effect is that most campaign communication goes from candidate to voter, with little feedback from voter to candidate. The more frequent use of polls in modern campaigns in part makes up for this one-way communicating pattern.

5. Leon V. Sigal, "Newsmen and Campaigners: Organization Men Make the News," *Political Science Quarterly* 93 (1978): 465-70.

6. Interview with J. Fred Coldren, August 17, 1977; and interview with Richard Leone, August 19, 1977.

7. See pp. 44-42

8. I owe this way of putting the point (although not the wording) to comments by James David Barber at a panel of the Midwest Political Science Association, Chicago, Illinois, April 21, 1978.

9. James M. Perry, "Loaded Guns and Other Weapons," in *The Political Image Merchants: Strategies in the New Politics,* ed. Ray E. Hiebert et al. (Washington, D.C.: Acropolis books, 1971), p. 216.

10. David H. Ostroff, "A Participant-Observer Study of TV Campaign Coverage," *Journalism Quarterly* 57 (1980): 417-18.

11. Interview with Mike McCarvile, June 25, 1980.

12. Garrett J. O'Keefe, "Political Campaigns and Mass Communication Research," in *Political Communication: Issues and Strategies for Research,* ed. Steven H. Chaffee (Beverly Hills, Calif.: Sage Publications, 1975), p. 130.

13. Ostroff, "A Participant-Observer Study," p. 417.

14. See, for instance, Wildavsky's description of one way to handle complexity in budgeting: "Another way of handling complexity is to use actions on simpler items as indices of more complicated ones. Instead of dealing directly with the cost of a huge atomic installation, for example, Congressmen may seek to discover how personnel and administrative costs or real estate transactions with which they have some familiarity are handled." Aaron Wildavsky, *The Politics of the Budgetary Process,* 2nd ed. (Boston: Little, Brown and Company, 1974), pp. 11-12. See Theodore H. White, *The Making of the President, 1960* (New York: Signet Books, 1961), pp. 374-80.

15. Robert Batlin, "San Francisco Newspapers' Campaign Coverage: 1896-1952," *Journalism Quarterly* 31 (1954): 297-303; Robert Bishop and Robert L. Brown, "Michigan Newspaper Bias in the 1966 Campaign," *Journalism Quarterly* 45 (1968): 337-38; Jules Witcover, "The Indiana Primary and the Indianapolis Newspapers— A Report in Detail," *Columbia Journalism Review* 7 (Summer 1968): 11-17.

16. Stanley Kelley, Jr., "Campaign Propaganda in Perspective," in *The President: Rex, Princeps, Imperator?* ed. Joseph M. Ray (El Paso, Tex.: Texas Western Press, 1969), p. 62.

17. Shadegg maximized the impact of gummed windshield stickers in the 1958 Barry Goldwater senatorial campaign in Arizona by distributing about a quarter of a million of them in five days to "heighten the impact tremendously." The sudden appearance of so many stickers "created an impression of strength out of all proportion to the actual number of stickers used." Stephen C. Shadegg, *How to Win an Election: The Art of Political Victory* (Arlington, Va.: Crestwood Books, 1964), pp. 67-70. The quotations are from pp. 69 and 70.

18. See the discussion of this release in chapter 4, pp. 60-61.

SELECTED BIBLIOGRAPHY

PUBLISHED SOURCES

Abrams, Mark. "Opinion Polls and Party Propaganda." *Public Opinion Quarterly* 28 (1964): 13-19.

Agranoff, Robert. *The Management of Election Campaigns.* Boston: Holbrook Press, 1976.

Albig, William. "Publicity, Advertising and Propaganda in the United States of America." *Gazette* 4 (1958): 23-32.

Allen, Frank. "News Releases from Business Irritate Editors." *Wall Street Journal,* May 20, 1981, p. 27.

Arrendell, Charles. "Predicting the Completeness of Newspaper Election Coverage." *Journalism Quarterly* 49 (1972): 290-95.

Atkin, Charles K. "How Imbalanced Campaign Coverage Affects Audience Exposure Patterns." *Journalism Quarterly* 48 (1971). 235-44.

Atkins, Chester G., with Barry Hock and Bob Martin. *Getting Elected: A Guide to Winning State and Local Office.* Boston: Houghton Mifflin Company, 1973.

Bagdikian, Ben H. "The Fruits of Agnewism." *Columbia Journalism Review* 11 (1973): 9-13, 15-21.

Bailey, George. "How Newsmakers Make the News." *Journal of Communication* 28 (1978): 80-83.

Barber, James David, ed. *Race for the Presidency: The Media and the Nominating Process.* Englewood Cliffs, N.J.: Prentice-Hall, 1978.

Barry, Brian M. *Sociologists, Economists and Democracy.* London: Collier-Macmillan, Ltd., 1970.

Bass, Abraham Z. "Refining the 'Gate-Keeper' Concept: A UN Radio Case Study." *Journalism Quarterly* 46 (1969): 69-72.

Batlin, Robert. "San Francisco Newspapers' Campaign Coverage: 1896-1952." *Journalism Quarterly* 31 (1954): 297-303.

Becker, Jerome D., and Ivan L. Preston. "Media Usage and Political Activity." *Journalism Quarterly* 46 (1969): 129-34.

Becker, Jules, and Douglas A. Fuchs. "How the Major California Dailies Covered Reagan vs. Brown." *Journalism Quarterly* 44 (1967): 645-53.

Becker, Lee B.; Maxwell E. McCombs; and Jack M. McLeod. "The Development of Political Cognitions." In *Political Communications: Issues and Strategies for Research.* Edited by Steven H. Chaffee, pp. 21-63. Beverly Hills, Calif.: Sage Publications, 1975.

Berres, Jean L. "The Daily Newspaper as a Channel of Information on Public Matters." *Journalism Quarterly* 48 (1971): 764-67.

Bishop, Robert, and Robert L. Brown. "Michigan Newspaper Bias in the 1966 Campaign." *Journalism Quarterly* 45 (1968): 337-38.

Block, Ralph. "Propaganda and the Free Society." *Public Opinion Quarterly* 12 (1948-1949): 677-86.

Blumberg, Nathan B. *One Party Press? Coverage of the 1952 Presidential Campaign in Thirty-Five Daily Newspapers.* Lincoln, Neb.: University of Nebraska Press, 1954.

Bogart, Leo. "Newspapers in the Age of Television." *Daedalus,* Winter 1963, pp. 116-27.

Bone, Hugh A. "Campaign Methods Today." *The Annals of the American Academy of Political and Social Science* 283 (1952): 127-40.

Bowers, David R. "A Report on Activity of Publishers in Directing Newsroom Decisions." *Journalism Quarterly* 44 (1967): 43-52.

Breed, Warren. "Analyzing News: Some Questions for Research." *Journalism Quarterly* 33 (1956): pp. 467-77.

Brown, James, and Philip M. Seib. *The Art of Politics: Electoral Strategies and Campaign Management.* Port Washington, N.Y.: Alfred Publishing Company, 1976.

Campbell, Angus; Philip E. Converse; Warren E. Miller; and Donald E. Stokes. *The American Voter.* New York: John Wiley & Sons, 1960.

―――. *Elections and the Political Order.* New York: John Wiley & Sons, 1966.

Cannon, James M., ed. *Politics, U.S.A.: A Practical Guide to the Winning of Public Office.* Garden City, N.Y.: Doubleday and Company, 1960.

Carter, John Franklin. *Power and Persuasion.* New York: Duell, Sloan and Pearce, 1960.

Carter, Richard F., and Bradley S. Greenberg. "Newspapers or Television: Which Do You Believe?" *Journalism Quarterly* 42 (1965): 29-34.

Carter, Roy E., Jr. "Newspaper 'Gatekeepers' and the Sources of News." *Public Opinion Quarterly* 22 (1958): 133-44.

Casey, Ralph D. "British Politics—Some Lessons in Campaign Propaganda." *Public Opinion Quarterly* 8 (1944): 72-83.

―――. "Party Campaign Propaganda." *The Annals of the American Academy of Political and Social Science* 179 (1935): 96-105.

Cater, Douglass. *The Fourth Branch of Government.* Boston: Houghton Mifflin Company, 1959.

Chaudhary, Anju. "Comparative News Judgment of Indian and American Journalists." *Gazette* 20 (1974): 233-47.

Clark, Peter, and Eric Fredin. "Newspapers, Television and Political Reasoning." *Public Opinion Quarterly* 42 (1978): 143-60.

Clem, Alan C. *The Making of Congressmen: Seven Campaigns of 1974.* North Scituate, Mass.: Duxbury Press, 1976.

Clor, Harry M., ed. *The Mass Media and Modern Democracy.* Chicago: Rand McNally, 1974.

Coblentz, Edmond D., ed. *Newsmen Speak: Journalists on Their Craft.* Berkeley, Calif.: University of California Press, 1954.

Cohen, Bernard C. *The Press and Foreign Policy.* Princeton, N.J.: Princeton University Press, 1963.

Colburn, John H. "Understanding the Role of the Press." *Nieman Reports,* no. 3 (1971): 13-16.

Crouse, Timothy. *The Boys on the Bus.* New York: Ballantine Books, 1973.

Danielson, Wayne, and John B. Adams. "Completeness of Press Coverage of the 1960 Campaign." *Journalism Quarterly* 38 (1961): 441-52.

Dawson, Paul A., and James E. Zinser. "Characteristics of Campaign Resource Allocation in the 1972 Congressional Elections." In *Changing Campaign Techniques: Elections and Values in Contemporary Democracies.* Edited by Louis Maisel, pp. 93-137. Beverly Hills, Calif.: Sage Publications, 1976.

Deckelnick, Gary. "The Candidate and the Media." *Campaign Insight* 9, no. 22 (November 15, 1978): 7-8.

De Fleur, Melvin L. *Theories of Mass Communication.* New York: David McKay Company, 1966.

Democratic State Committee of New Jersey. *Election Workshop Manual: The Communications Handbook.* Trenton, N.J., no date.

De Vries, Walter, and Lance Tarrance, Jr. *The Ticket-Splitter: A New Face in American Politics.* Grand Rapids, Mich.: William B. Eerdmans Publishing Company, 1972.

Dexter, Lewis Anthony. "Candidates Must Make the Issues and Give Them Meaning." *Public Opinion Quarterly* 19 (1950): 408-14.

Donohew, Lewis. "Newspaper Gatekeepers and Forces in the News Channel." *Public Opinion Quarterly* 31 (1967): 61-68.

Dovring, Karin. "The Community Context in Political Newswriting." *PROD* 2 (1958): 6-8.

Downs, Anthony. *An Economic Theory of Democracy.* New York: Harper & Row, 1957.

Dunn, Delmer D. *Public Officials and the Press.* Reading, Mass.: Addison-Wesley Publishing Company, 1969.

Eldersveld, Samuel J. "Experimental Propaganda Techniques and Voting

Behavior." *American Political Science Review* 45 (1956): 154-65.

Ellul, Jacques. *Propaganda: The Formation of Men's Attitudes.* Translated from the French by Konrad Keller and Jean Lerner. New York: Alfred A. Knopf, 1965.

Emery, Edwin. "Changing Role of the Mass Media in American Politics." *The Annals of the American Academy of Political and Social Science* 427 (1976): 84-94.

Erickson, Robert S. "The Advantage of Incumbency in Congressional Elections." *Polity* 3 (1971): 395-405.

Evarts, Dru, and Guido H. Stempel, III. "Coverage of the 1972 Campaign by TV, News Magazine and Major Newspapers." *Journalism Quarterly* 51 (1974): 645-48, 676.

Ferguson, LeRoy C., and Ralph H. Smuckler. *Politics in the Press: An Analysis of Press Content in 1952 Senatorial Campaigns.* East Lansing, Mich.: The Government Research Bureau, Michigan State College, 1954.

FitzPatrick, Dick. "Measuring Government Publicity: Volume of Press Releases." *Journalism Quarterly* 26 (1949): 45-50.

———. "Public Information Activities of Government Agencies." *Public Opinion Quarterly* 11 (1947): 530-39.

Ford, James L. C., and Howard R. Long. "Professional Standards for a Professional Press." *Grassroots Editor* 5, no. 4 (1964): 7-8, 38.

Freimuth, Vicki S., and J. Paul Van Nevel. "Reaching the Public: The Asbestos Awareness Campaign." *Journal of Communication* 31 (1981): 155-67.

Frost, Richard T. "Stability and Change in Local Party Politics." *Public Opinion Quarterly* 25 (1961): 221-35.

Gaby, Daniel M., and Merle H. Treusch. *Election Campaign Handbook.* Englewood Cliffs, N.J.: Prentice-Hall, 1976).

Gans, Herbert J. *Deciding What's News: A Study of CBS Evening News, NBC Nightly News, Newsweek, and Time.* New York: Pantheon Books, 1979.

Ghiglinoe, Loren, ed. *Evaluating the Press: The New England Daily Newspper Survey.* Southbridge, Mass.: New England Daily Newspaper Survey, 1973.

Gieber, Walter. "Across the Desk: A Study of 16 Telegraph Editors." *Journalism Quarterly* 33 (1956): 423-32.

Glick, Edward M. *The Federal Government-Daily Press Relationship.* Washington, D.C.: The American Institute for Political Communication, 1967.

Gosnell, Harold F. "Does Campaigning Make a Difference?" *Public Opinion Quarterly* 14 (1950): 413-18.

Graber, Doris A. *Mass Media and American Politics.* Washington, D.C.: CQ Press, 1980.

Gregg, James E. "Newspaper Editorial Endorsements and California Elections, 1948-1962." *Journalism Quarterly* 42 (1965): 532-38.

Grossman, Michael Baruch, and Francis E. Rourke. "The Media and the Presidency." *Political Science Quarterly* 91 (1976): 455-70.

Grossman, Michael Baruch, and Martha Joynt Kumar. *Portraying the President: The White House and the News Media.* Baltimore: Johns Hopkins University Press, 1981.

Harris, David H. "Publicity Releases: Why They End Up in the Wastebasket." *Industrial Marketing* 46 (June 1961): 98-100.

Hart, Jim A. "Election Campaign Coverage in English and U.S. Daily Newspapers." *Journalism Quarterly* 42 (1965): 213-18.

Hemanus, Petri. "Propaganda and Indoctrination: A Tentative Concept Analysis." *Gazette* 20 (1974): 215-23.

―――. "A Short Reply to Kjell Nowak." *Gazette* 21 (1975): 42-43.

Hiebart, Eldon, ed. *The Press in Washington.* New York: Dodd, Mead and Company, 1966.

Hiebert, Ray E. et al., eds. *The Political Image Merchants: Strategies in the New Politics.* Washington, D.C.: Acropolis Books, 1971.

―――. *The Political Image Merchants: Strategies for the Seventies.* Washington, D.C.: Acropolis Books, 1975.

Higbie, Charles E. "Wisconsin Dailies in the 1952 Campaign: Space vs. Display." *Journalism Quarterly* 31 (1954): 56-60.

Hixson, Richard F. "A Brief Look at New Jersey's Prosperous Daily Press. *Journalism Quarterly* 43 (1966): 765-69.

Hohenberg, John. *The Professional Journalist.* 2nd ed. New York: Holt, Rinehart and Winston, 1969.

Holsti, Ole R. *Content Analysis for the Social Sciences and Humanities.* Reading, Mass.: Addison-Wesley Publishing Company, 1969.

Hooper, Michael. "Party and Newspaper Endorsements as Predictors of Voter Choice." *Journalism Quarterly* 46 (1969): 302-5.

Huckshorn, Robert J., and Robert C. Spencer. *The Politics of Defeat: Campaigning for Congress.* Amherst, Mass.: University of Massachusetts Press, 1971.

Janowitz, Morris. "Professional Models in Journalism: The Gatekeeper and the Advocate." *Journalism Quarterly* 52 (1975): 618-26, 662.

Jennings, M. Kent, and L. Harmon Zeigler, eds. *The Electoral Process.* Englewood Cliffs, N.J.: Prentice-Hall, 1966.

Kaid, Lynda Lee. "Newspaper Treatment of a Candidate's News Releases." *Journalism Quarterly* 53 (1976): 135-37.

―――, Keith R. Sanders, and Robert O. Hirsch. *Political Campaign Communication: A Bibliography and Guide to the Literature.* Metuchen, N.J.: The Scarecrow Press, 1974.

Kayden, Xandra. "The Political Campaign as Organization." *Public Policy* 21 (1973): 263-90.

Kelley, Stanley, Jr. "Campaign Propaganda in Perspective." In *The President: Rex, Princeps, Imperator?* Edited by Joseph M. Ray, pp. 59-67. El Paso, Tex.: Texas Western Press, 1969.

―――. *Political Campaigning: Problems in Creating an Informed Electorate.* Washington, D.C.: The Brookings Institution, 1960.

―――. *Professional Public Relations and Political Power.* Baltimore: John Hopkins Press, 1956.

Kerrick, Jean S. "The Inverted Pyramid Style and Attitude Change." *Journalism Quarterly* 36 (1959): 479-82.

Key, V. O., Jr. *Politics, Parties, and Pressure Groups.* 5th ed. New York: Thomas Y. Crowell Company, 1964.

Kingdon, John W. *Candidates for Office: Beliefs and Strategies.* New York: Random House, 1966.

Lang, Gladys E., and Kurt Lang. "The Inferential Structure of Political Communications: A Study in Unwitting Bias." *Public Opinion Quarterly* 19 (1955-56): 168-83.

Lasswell, Harold D. "The Theory of Political Propaganda." *American Political Science Review* 21 (1929): 627-31.

Lazarsfeld, Paul; Bernard Berelson; and Hazel Gaudet. *The People's Choice: How the Voter Makes Up His Mind in a Presidential Campaign.* 3rd ed. New York: Columbia University Press, 1968.

Lee, Richard, ed. *Politics and the Press.* Washington, D.C.: Acropolis Books, 1970.

Leubsdorf, Carl P. "The Reporter and the Presidential Candidate." *The Annals of the American Academy of Political and Social Science* 427 (1976): 1-11.

Leuthold, David A. *Electioneering in a Democracy: Campaigns for Congress.* New York: John Wiley & Sons, 1968.

Lippman, Walter. *Public Opinion.* New York: Haarcourt, Brace and Company, 1922.

Lumsdaine, Arthur A., and Irving L. Janis. "Resistance to 'Counterpropaganda' Produced by One-Sided and Two-Sided 'Propaganda' Presentations." *Public Opinion Quarterly* 17 (1953): 311-18.

Manheim, Jarol B. "Urbanization and Differential Press Coverage of the Congressional Campaign." *Journalism Quarterly* 51 (1974): 649-53, 669.

Martin, L. John. "Recent Theory on Mass Media Potential in Political Campaigns." *The Annals of the American Academy of Political and Social Science* 427 (1976): 125-33.

Martin, William P., and Michael W. Singletary. "Newspaper Treatment of State Government Releases." *Journalism Quarterly* 58 (1981): 93-96.

Mason, William. "The Impact of Endorsements on Voting." *Sociological Methods and Research* 1 (1973): 463-95.

May, Ernest R., and Janet Fraser. *Campaign '73: The Managers Speak.* Cambridge, Mass.: Harvard University Press, 1973.

Mayo, Charles G. "The Mass Media and Campaign Strategy in a Mayoralty Election." *Journalism Quarterly* 41 (1964): 353-59.

McClunghan, Jack Sean. "Effect of Endorsements in Texas Local Elections." *Journalism Quarterly* 50 (1973): 362-66.

McCombs, Maxwell E. "Editorial Endorsements: A Study of Influence." *Journalism Quarterly* 44 (1967): 545-48.

———, and Donald R. Shaw. "The Agenda-Setting Function of Mass Media." *Public Opinion Quarterly* 36 (1972): 176-87.

McDowell, James L. "The Role of Newspapers in Illinois At-Large Election." *Journalism Quarterly* 42 (1965): 176-87.

McGuire, William J., and Demetrios Papegeorgis. "Effectiveness of Forewarning in Developing Resistance to Persuasion." *Public Opinion Quarterly* 26 (1962): 24-34.

Merrill, John C., and Ralph D. Barney, eds. *Ethics and the Press: Readings in Mass Media Morality.* New York: Hastings House Publishers, 1975.

Miller, Susan H. "News Coverage of Congress: The Search for the Ultimate Spokesman." *Journalism Quarterly* 54 (1977): 459-65.

Mueller, John E. "Choosing Among 133 Candidates." *Public Opinion Quarterly* 34 (1970-71): 395-402.

Mullen, James J. "How Candidates for the Senate Use Newspaper Advertising." *Journalism Quarterly* 40 (1963): 532-38.

Napolitan, Joseph. "Media Costs and Effects in Political Campaigns." *The Annals of the American Academy of Political and Social Science* 427 (1976): 114-24.

Nicolai, Richard R., and Sam G. Riley. "The Gatekeeping Function from the Point of View of the PR Man." *Journalism Quarterly* 49 (1972): 371-73.

Nimmo, Dan D. *Newsgathering in Washington: A Study in Political Communication.* New York: Atherton Press, 1964.

———. "Political Image Makers and the Mass Media." *The Annals of the American Academy of Political and Social Science* 427 (1976): 33-44.

———. *The Political Persuaders: The Techniques of Modern Election Campaigns.* Englewood Cliffs, N.J.: Prentice-Hall, 1970.

———, and Robert L. Savage. *Candidates and Their Images: Concepts, Methods, and Findings.* Pacific Palisades, Calif.: Goodyear Publishing Company, 1976.

Nowak, Kjell. "'Propaganda and Indoctrination: A Tentative Concept Analysis' by Petri Hemanus." *Gazette* 21 (1975): 40-42.

O'Keefe, Garrett J. "Political Campaigns and Mass Communication Research." In *Political Communication: Issues and Strategies for Re-*

search. Edited by Steven H. Chaffee, pp. 129-64. Beverly Hills, Calif.: Sage Publications, 1975.

Ostroff, David H. "A Participant-Observer Study of TV Campaign Coverage." *Journalism Quarterly* 57 (1980): 415-19.

Paletz, David L. "Candidates and the Media in the 1976 Presidential Election." In *Parties and Elections in an Anti-Party Age: American Politics and the Crisis of Confidence.* Edited by Jeff Fishel, pp. 256-62. Bloomington, Ind.: Indiana University Press, 1978.

Patterson, Thomas E., and Robert D. McClure. *The Unseeing Eye: The Myth of Television Power in National Politics.* New York: G. P. Putnam's Sons, 1976.

Pearlin, Leonard J., and Morris Rosenberg. "Propaganda Techniques in Institutional Advertising." *Public Opinion Quarterly* 32 (1968): 95-101.

Perry, James M. *The New Politics: The Expanding Technology of Political Manipulation.* New York: Clarkson N. Potter, 1968.

Pohl, Frederik. *Practical Politics 1972: How to Make Politics and Politicians Work for You.* New York: Ballantine Books, 1971.

Polk, Leslie D.; John Eddy; and Ann Andre. "Use of Congressional Publicity in Wisconsin District." *Journalism Quarterly* 52 (1975): 543-46.

Polsby, Nelson W., and Aaron Wildavsky. *Presidential Elections: Strategies of American Electoral Politics.* 4th ed. New York: Charles Scribner's Sons, 1976.

Pomper, Gerald, with colleagues. *The Election of 1980.* Chatham, N.J.: Chatham House Publishers, 1981.

Pool, Ithiel de Sola, and Irwin Shulman. "Newsmen's Fantasies, Audiences, and Newswriting." *Public Opinion Quarterly* 31 (1954): 447-58.

Price, G. "A Method for Analyzing Newspaper Campaign Coverage." *Journalism Quarterly* 31 (1954): 447-58.

Pye, Lucian W., ed. *Communication and Political Development.* Princeton, N.J.: Princeton University Press, 1963.

Repass, David E., and Steven Chaffee. "Administrative vs. Campaign Coverage of Two Presidents in Eight Partisan Dailies." *Journalism Quarterly* 45 (1968): 528-31.

Rings, Robert L. "Public School News Coverage With and Without PR Directors." *Journalism Quarterly* 48 (1971): 62-67, 72.

Rivers, William L. *The Adversaries: Politics and the Press.* Boston: Beacon Press, 1970.

Robinson, John P. "Perceived Media Bias and the 1968 Vote: Can the Media Affect Behavior After All?" *Journalism Quarterly* 49 (1972): 239-46.

———. "The Press and the Voter," *The Annals of the American Academy of Political and Social Science* 427 (1976): 95-103.

———. "The Press as King-Maker: What Surveys From Last Five Campaigns Show." *Journalism Quarterly* 51 (1974): 587-94, 606.

Rosenbloom, David Lee. *The Election Men: Professional Campaign Managers and American Democracy.* New York: Quadrangle Books, 1973.
————. "The Press and the Local Candidate." *The Annals of the American Academy of Political and Social Science* 427 (1976): 12-22.
Roshco, Bernard. *Newsmaking.* Chicago: University of Chicago Press, 1975.
Rosnow, Ralph L. "One-Sided Versus Two-Sided Communications Under Indirect Awareness of Persuasive Intent." *Public Opinion Quarterly* 32 (1968): 95-101.
Rosten, Leo C. *The Washington Correspondents.* New York: Arno Press, 1974.
Schwartzman, Edward. *Campaign Craftsmanship: A Professional's Guide to Campaigning for Elective Office.* New York: Universe Books, 1972.
Shadegg, Stephen C. *How to Win an Election: The Art of Political Victory.* Arlington, Va.: Crestwood Books, 1964.
Shelton, Keith. "Timeliness in the News: Television vs. Newspapers." *Journalism Quarterly* 55 (1978): 348-50.
Siebert, Fred S. et al. *Four Theories of the Press.* Urbana, Ill.: University of Illinois Press, 1956.
Sigal, Leon V. "Newsmen and Campaigners: Organization Men Make the News." *Political Science Quarterly* 93 (1978): 465-70.
Smith, Bruce L. "Propaganda," *International Encyclopedia of the Social Sciences.* New York: Macmillan and The Free Press, 1968, Vol. 12, p. 579-89.
Smith, Charles W., Jr. "Campaign Communication Media." *The Annals of the American Academy of Political and Social Science* 259 (1948): 90-97.
Spector, N. J. "The Impact of the Editorial Page on a Municipal Referendum," *Journalism Quarterly* 47 (1970): 762-66.
Staff of the *New York Times, The Newspaper: Its Making and Its Meaning.* New York: Charles Scribner's Sons, 1955.
Steinberg, Arnold. *The Political Campaign Handbook: Media, Scheduling, and Advance.* Lexington, Mass.: Lexington Books, 1976.
Swerdlow, Joel. "The Decline of the Boys on the Bus." *Washington Journalism Review* 3, no. 1 (1981): 15-19.
Tedin, Kent L., and Richard W. Murray. "Dynamics of Candidate Choice in a State Election." *Journal of Politics* 43 (1981): 435-55.
Thompson, Dennis F. "Rational Propaganda." *Public Policy* 15 (1966): 86-115.
Thomson, Charles A. H. *Television and Presidential Poltics: The Experience in 1952 and the Problems Ahead.* Washington, D.C.: The Brookings Institution, 1956.
Thomson, James C., Jr. "Government and Press." *Nieman Reports* 27, no. 4 (1973): 32-34, 36-38.
Tichenor, Philip J.; Charia N. Olien; and George A. Donohue. "Pre-

dicting a Source's Success in Placing News in the Media." *Journalism Quarterly* 44 (1967): 32-42.

Tufte, Edward R. "Improving Data Analysis in Political Science." *World Politics* 21 (1969): 641-54.

Van Riper, Paul. *Handbook of Practical Politics.* New York: Harper & Row, 1967.

Vinyard, Dale, and Roberta S. Sigel. "Newspapers and Urban Voters." *Journalism Quarterly* 48 (1971): 486-93.

Westley, Bruce H., and Malcolm S. MacLean, Jr. "A Conceptual Model for Communications Research." *Journalism Quarterly* 34 (1957): 31-38.

White, David Manning. "The 'Gate-Keeper': A Case Study in the Selection of News." *Journalism Quarterly* 27 (1950): 283-90.

Wiggins, J. Russell. " 'The Facts Are What Matter.' " *Neman Reports* 15, no. 1 (1971): 15-18.

Wilhoit, G. Cleveland, and Taik Sup Auh. "Newspaper Endorsement and Coverage of Public Opinion Polls in 1970." *Journalism Quarterly* 51 (1974): 654-58.

Winhauser, John W. "Content Patterns of Editorials in Ohio Metropolitan Dailies." *Journalism Quarterly* 50 (1973): 562-67.

Witcover, Jules. "The Indiana Primary and the Indianapolis Newspapers— A Report in Detail." *Columbia Journalism Review* 7 (Summer 1968): 11-17.

————. *Marathon: The Pursuit of the Presidency, 1972-1976.* New York: The Viking Press, 1977.

UNPUBLISHED SOURCES

Bolen, John H. "Daily Newspaper Coverage of the 1970 Texas Gubernatorial Campaign." M.A. thesis, University of Texas, 1970.

Calvert, Leonard James. "A Survey of Use of Extension Agent News Releases in Six Oregon Counties." M.A. thesis, University of Oregon, 1976.

Felzenberg, Alvin Stephen. "The Impact of Gubernatorial Style on Policy Outcomes: An In Depth Study of Three New Jersey Governors." Ph.D. dissertation, Princeton University, 1978.

Gale, Gary. "The Operation of a Political Press Office in a Mayoral Election in a Major American City." M.A. thesis, University of Missouri-Columbia, 1976.

Miller, James. "Usage of News Releases from California State University, Fresno, by Selected Daily and Weekly Newspapers." M.A. thesis, California State University, Fresno, 1977.

Millwood, Sharron Smith. "A Content Analysis of Extension-Prepared

News Appearing in Selected Georgia Weeklies." M.A. thesis, University of Georgia, 1975.
Paul, Bene Louise. "Media Use in a California Assembly Campaign: A Case Study." M.A. thesis, San Jose State University, 1976.

INTERVIEWS

Besler, Max, November 24, 1980.
Coldren, J. Fred, August 17, 1977.
Forsythe, Kathy, August 16, 1977.
Hunter, Harold V., June 25, 1980.
Johnson, Judy, November 25, 1980.
Leone, Richard, August 19, 1977.
Matthews, Steven, November 20, 1980.
McCarvile, Mike, June 25, 1980.
Stromberger, Ernie, June 23, 1980.
Todd, Reginald, June 19, 1980.
Towns, Leroy, March 13, 1981.
Wolfe, Herbert, July 10, 1975.

INDEX

About the Author

JAN PONS VERMEER is Associate Professor and Head of the
Department of Political Science at Nebraska Wesleyan University
in Lincoln, Nebraska. He specializes in the study of the media and
American politics.